MIS Cases

Solving Small Business Case Scenarios Using Application Software

Second Edition

CYNTHIA GARDNER
University of San Diego

EUGENE RATHSWOHL
University of San Diego

WILEY

VP & EXECUTIVE PUBLISHER:	Don Fowley
EXECUTIVE EDITOR:	Beth Lang Golub
ASSISTANT EDITOR:	Samantha Mandel
MARKETING MANAGER:	Christopher Ruel
MARKETING ASSISTANT:	Ashley Tomeck
DESIGNER:	Kenji Ngieng
SENIOR PRODUCTION MANAGER:	Janis Soo
ASSOCIATE PRODUCTION MANAGER:	Joyce Poh
COVER CREDITS:	©Henrik Jonsson/iStockphoto

This book was set by Laserwords Private Limited. Cover and text printed and bound by Malloy Lithographers.

This book is printed on acid free paper.

Founded in 1807, John Wiley & Sons, Inc. has been a valued source of knowledge and understanding for more than 200 years, helping people around the world meet their needs and fulfill their aspirations. Our company is built on a foundation of principles that include responsibility to the communities we serve and where we live and work. In 2008, we launched a Corporate Citizenship Initiative, a global effort to address the environmental, social, economic, and ethical challenges we face in our business. Among the issues we are addressing are carbon impact, paper specifications and procurement, ethical conduct within our business and among our vendors, and community and charitable support. For more information, please visit our website: www.wiley.com/go/citizenship.

Evaluation copies are provided to qualified academics and professionals for review purposes only, for use in their courses during the next academic year. These copies are licensed and may not be sold or transferred to a third party. Upon completion of the review period, please return the evaluation copy to Wiley. Return instructions and a free-of-charge return mailing label are available at www.wiley.com/go/returnlabel. If you have chosen to adopt this textbook for use in your course, please accept this book as your complimentary desk copy. Outside of the United States, please contact your local sales representative.

Library of Congress Cataloging-in-Publication Data

Gardner, Cynthia, 1971-
  MIS cases: solving small business-scenarios using application software /
Cynthia Gardner, Eugene Rathswohl.
    p. cm.
  Includes index.
  ISBN 978-1-118-29161-0 (pbk.)
  1. Management information systems. 2. Small business—Data processing. 3. Information technology—Management. I. Rathswohl, Eugene J. II. Title.
  HD30.213.G367 2013
  658.4'038011—dc23

                    2012022850

Printed in the United States of America

10 9 8 7 6 5 4 3

Preface

This book is designed as a supplement for an information systems or information technology introductory course. It contains 22 small business case scenarios that will help your students understand the use of database applications, spreadsheet applications, and Web design.

The book has seven chapters, with three cases in each chapter. Cases 1 through 9 are Access database small business scenarios. There is an additional capstone case in Access. Cases 10 through 18 are Excel spreadsheet scenarios. Cases 19 through 21 are website design scenarios. The cases have been designed to fit into a one-hour instructor demonstration.

The first case in every chapter is used as a teaching case to be demonstrated to your students during class. The second and third cases match the skill set of the demonstrated teaching case, allowing the students to practice what they have learned in these additional assignment cases. These small business cases include tracking business revenue within multiple stores, projecting the cost of remodeling a restaurant, managing inventory in a chiropractic office using a client database, and many other scenarios. The skill level for each set of cases progresses from beginning to intermediate to advanced. The capstone case in Access encompasses the majority of skills taught in the previous Access cases.

BREAKDOWN OF CASE DESIGN

The cases in the book have a consistent design that begins with a preview of the small business scenario, skill level, and background. The cases include case specifications, design, and implementation. There are questions at the end of each case.

Preview gives a quick synopsis of the small business case and what is to be accomplished in the case.

Skill Set is a listing of the skills that are taught in the case and the skills that are duplicated in the assignment cases to follow.

Background gives a complete description and expanded explanation of the goal to be completed at the end of the small business scenario.

Case Analysis includes three requirements:

- Output Requirements are a description of the completed goal of the scenario.

- Input Requirements are instructions for inputting information that is needed to begin the scenario.

- Processing Requirements are the set of instructions on how to complete the case study.

Design and Implementation gives instructions on the design aspects and proper formatting of the scenario for completing the case specifications.

Using the Application allows the students to use the application as a tool to answer questions and solve problems. The goal is to have the students shift from designer of the application to the end user of the application.

▶ SUPPLEMENTS

This text is accompanied by Instructor and Student files. The instructor files are the completed cases and the student files are a starter kit for each case. The answers to the questions for the Excel files are included in the Instructor file on an additional sheet in the Excel workbook. The answers to the questions for the Access files are included as a Word document. There are no Instructor files for the Web component.

If you have any questions or comments about the book, please e-mail Cynthia Gardner-Nitsch at cnitsch@sandiego.edu.

▶ ACKNOWLEDGEMENTS

We are grateful for the support of multiple people through the process of completing this second edition. We would like to thank Executive Editor Beth Golub and Assistant Editor Samantha Mandel for helping us complete this book. We would like to especially thank our book representative Brian Hinshaw, who initially invited us to write this book.

We would like to thank the reviewers for this book, from whom we received great suggestions and feedback:

Sherry Grosso, University of South Carolina at Sumter
Gina M. Jones, Aims Community College
Elizabeth Baker, Wake Forest University
Carol Wysocki, Columbia Basin Community College

To Mike and Max
Cynthia Gardner-Nitsch

To Sheila Anthony
E.J.R.

Contents

DEVELOPING A DATABASE APPLICATION

A database application is a software tool to keep track of data used in a business process, such as inventory control and customer relations. Think of a database application as an organized collection of information (tables) about the various entities (such as products, customers, and employees) of a business that allows the users to retrieve, analyze, and display the information to answer questions. Database applications are very important in managing today's organizations, providing professionals an effective way of managing their information resources and supporting their decision-making needs.

You should follow a three-phase approach to create a database application: analysis, design, and implementation.

In the analysis phase, you need to understand as well as you can the intended purpose of the database application, especially the desired output (reports). Importantly, you need to identify the desired attributes, or characteristics, for each of the entities to be stored in the database tables. You need to identify the desired queries to perform to retrieve desired information from the database tables. Also, you need to identify the reports the user desires. Each of the following cases presents the input, processing, and output requirements; in the real world you would determine these requirements through interviews with the intended users of the database application.

In the design phase, you need to decide how to lay out the data tables, the forms the user might need for entering the data into the tables, the queries to use, and the reports identified in your analysis. A well-designed database application is easy to use and produces correct results. There are many design guidelines you can follow to make sure the input and output features are clear and easy to use and the queries are correct. These design guidelines are discussed briefly as you go through the database cases.

During the implementation phase you use a database program, such as Access, to actually create the database application electronically. In the following database cases, you use Access to create the input files, the queries, and the various report files and to apply value-added design features to improve the usability of the database. Very importantly, you need to edit your database by correcting any mistakes, especially in the input files. Several coding, editing, and documentation approaches are discussed briefly in the following database cases.

After the database application is developed, users employ it to support their decision making. Often a user wants to search, or query, the database to retrieve information to answer new questions, referred to as data mining. Several data-mining techniques are discussed briefly in the database cases.

CHAPTER 1

Access—Tables and Forms

Up the Hill Bakery

Inventory and Customer Database

ACCESS TEACHING CASE: BEGINNING LEVEL

Submission Instructions   Complete Case 1 in Access. Answer the questions at the end of this case and ask your instructor for submission instructions.

Preview   You are the restaurant manager of the bakery and you need to create a simple database with two tables using two data entry forms. As the manager you need to keep track of the bakery's inventory and customer contact information. At the end of this case you will be able to create two tables with various field properties and create an easy-to-use input form for each table.

Skill Set

Table Design	Form Design
Field properties	Command buttons
Lookup Wizard	Calculated fields
Validation rule	Page formatting
Validation text	
Input mask	

Background You are the restaurant manager of a small French bakery in Chula Vista, California. Your customers are local residents and other small restaurants around the city. The bakery delivers fresh bread and pastries to customers; breakfast and lunch are also served within the store. The bakery doesn't bake all their items; some great chefs around the area drop off their specialties as well. As restaurant manager you need to keep track of the bakery's inventory, especially between which items are made in the store and which items come from other chefs. You also need to properly keep track of the daily deliveries and accounting issues with each account.

▶ CASE ANALYSIS

Output Requirements

Up the Hill Bakery needs a database application consisting of two tables: an Inventory table and a Customer table. They also need two input forms based on these tables for easy data entry and editing. You are to create this database from a blank database and save it as Up the Hill Bakery database.

Input Requirements

Jack and Susan need to record and store information about each of the inventory items. The attribute information for each inventory item includes the item identification number, item name, item type, whether the item is made in the bakery, the supplier's name (if any), the average number sold per day, and the price per item, as shown in Table 1.1.

You will need a data-entry form to enter or modify the data for each inventory item in the table quickly and accurately. Using the same fields as in the table, include item identification number, item name, item type, whether the item is made in the bakery, the supplier name (if any), and the average number sold per day, and the price per item.

Similarly, the attribute information you want to store in the Customer table includes each customer's identification number, customer type, first name, last name, street address, city, and zip code as shown in Table 1.2. Use a data-entry form to enter or modify the data for each customer in the Customer table.

Table 1.1   Inventory Table

Item Id	Item Name	Item Type	Made in Store	Supplier Name	Daily Average Number Sold	Price Per Item
B111	Blueberry & Apricot	Pastry	Yes		12	3.95
B211	Pick Me Up	Drink	No	Flower Juice Co.	10	2.95
B311	Spicy Olive	Bread	Yes		5	6.00

Table 1.2 Customer Table

Customer ID	Customer Type	First Name	Last Name	Address	City	Zip	Phone Number
C123	Office building	Max	Nitsch	3205 Ridgecrest Dr.	Bonita	91902	(619) 867-0987
C124	Individual	Stephanie	Baker	2543 Gray St	La Jolla	92110	(858) 657-4987
C125	Restaurant	Katherine	Haupt	8425 Calle Adolanto	San Diego	92123	(760) 538-5453

▶ DESIGN AND IMPLEMENTATION

Inventory Table and Customer Table

Design Principle

Each field of information in a table represents an attribute of the entities being stored in the table; the fields should be named clearly and arranged logically. There should be one field, called the primary key field, that uniquely identifies each record, usually by a unique identification code.

Figure 1.1 shows the Inventory table properties. The columns represent the fields of information, and each row depicts a record for each item of inventory.

Implementation

Inventory Table

1. ItemId is a primary key; it consists of exactly four characters; all item IDs should start with a "B" and end with three digits. Use validation rules and validation text to complete this step. See Figure 1.1 to verify the field properties. ItemId field should

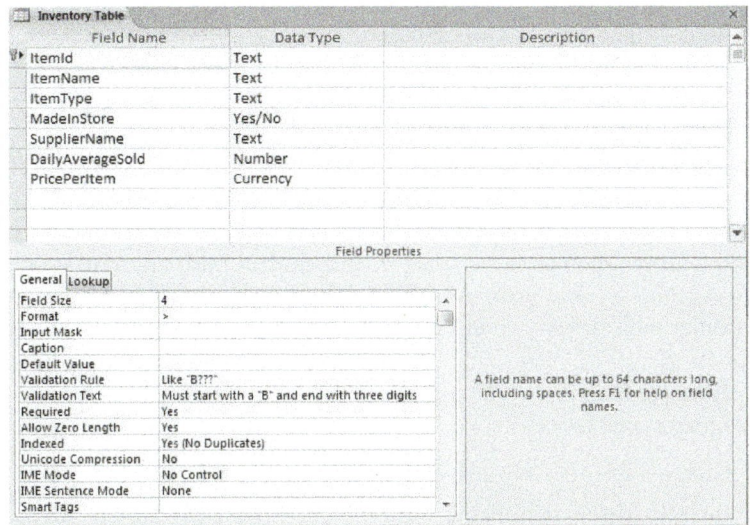

Figure 1.1 ItemId; Primary Key Field Properties

have a format field property that indicates the format should be all capital letters and that it is a required field.

2. ItemName should only have a field size of 30.

3. Create a Lookup Wizard for ItemType; Bread, Specialty Drink, Pastry Item.

4. MadeinStore field is a Yes/No data type with a default answer of Yes.

5. SupplierName should have a field size of 30.

6. DailyAverageSold should have a data type of number.

7. PriceOfItem should be a Currency format with two decimal places.

8. Save the table as Inventory and enter the three records as shown in Table 1.1.

Customer Table

1. CustomerId is a primary key. It should consist of exactly four characters: All customer IDs start with a "C" for Customer and end with three digits. Use validation rules and validation text to complete this step.

2. The CustomerId field should have a format field property of the greater than symbol, which indicates all capital letters. CustomerId is a required field.

3. Create a Lookup Wizard for the CustomerType field: Individual, Restaurant, Office.

4. The field properties for the FirstName and LastName fields should have a character size of 15.

5. Create a Lookup Wizard for the City field: San Diego, Del Mar, La Jolla, Bonita.

6. The Address field should have a field size of 40.

7. Use the Zip Code input mask for the Zip field.

8. Use the Phone number input mask for the PhoneNumber field.

9. Save the table as Customer and enter the three records that can be found in Table 1.2.

Inventory Input Form and Customer Input Form

Design Principle

Database application users can more accurately enter and modify information in database tables if they use predesigned data-entry forms. The form layout can include visual features such as titles, images, and control buttons to make adding and deleting information easy and error-free. The data entry forms for the Inventory table and the Customer table are shown in Figure 1.2 and Figure 1.3 on the following pages.

Implementation

Inventory Input Form

1. Create a Form in Wizard for your Inventory table, and include all the fields.

2. Include three command buttons: Add Record, Delete Record, Close Form. Name your buttons properly according to the form you are designing, i.e., CustomerFormAdd, CustomerFormDelete, CustomerFormClose.

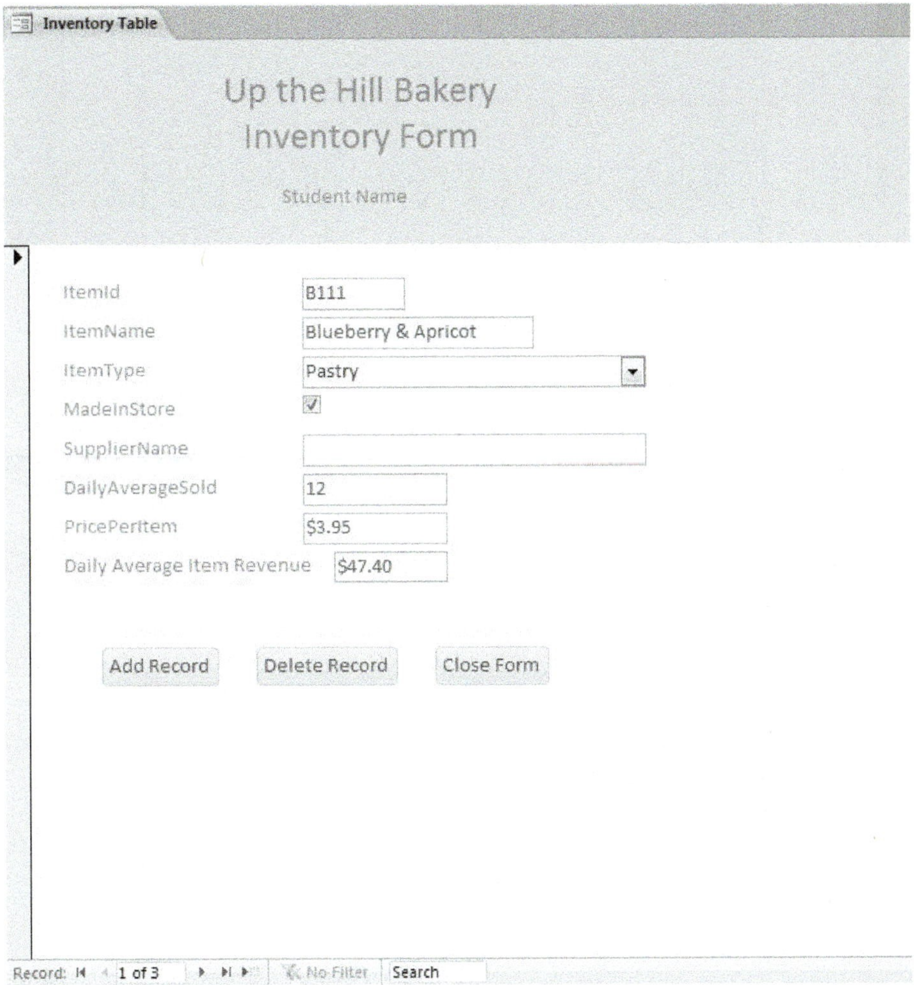

Figure 1.2 Inventory Form

3. Insert a proper form title (don't forget to use the label icon!).
4. Include an additional label within the header with your first and last name.
5. Choose a different color for the header and the detail section.
6. Include a calculated field to determine the daily average revenue of an item. (Hint: [Daily Average Sold] * [Price Of Item].)
7. Add a new record to the database. Create all the information on your own.

Customer Input Form

1. Create the Customer form in Wizard for your Customer table.
2. Follow steps 2 through 4 from the Inventory input form.

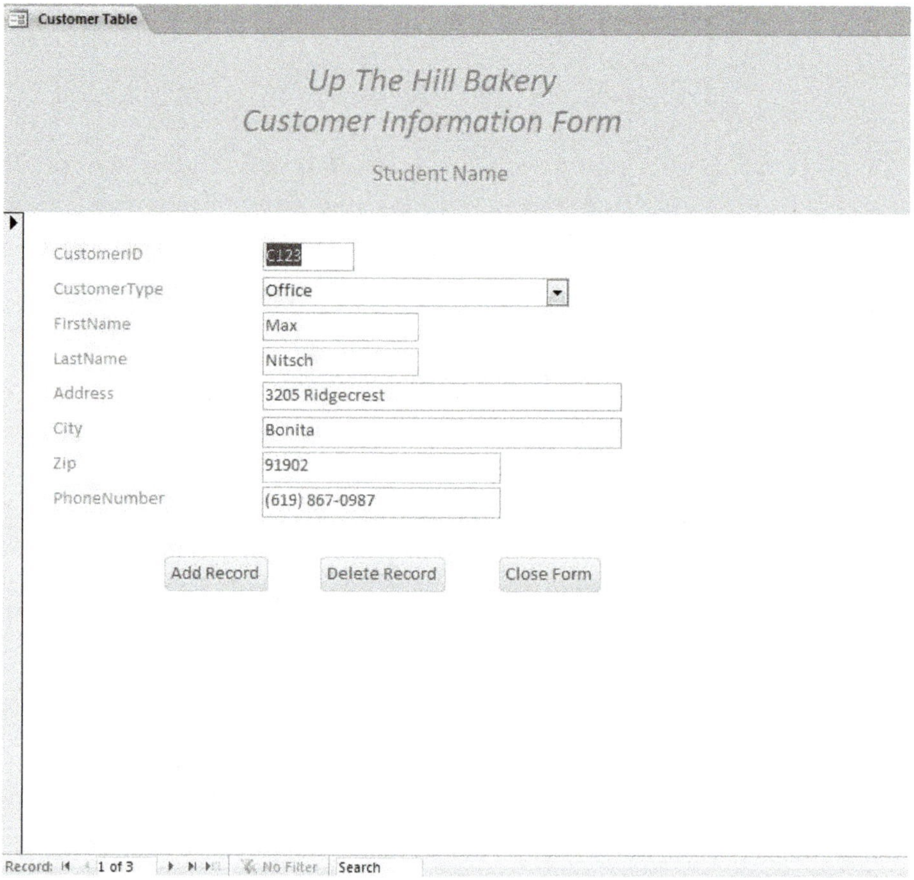

Figure 1.3 Customer Form

3. Add a new record to the database. Create all the information on your own.
4. Save the form.

▶ USING THE DATABASE APPLICATION

1. Organizing information into database tables underlies the effective use of information by Up the Hill Bakery.

   a. Why are two tables—the Customer table and the Inventory table—used in the bakery's database? Why not just use one table?

   b. What is the purpose of each field in each of the two tables? Why is it important to specify the field properties for each field in the tables?

   c. What is the purpose of the primary key in each of the two tables? Why is it necessary to have a primary key?

2. Entering accurate customer and inventory information into the database is critical for Up the Hill Bakery.

   a. Overall, why does using the customer and inventory input forms increase the accuracy of information in the database?

   b. Why do the validation rule and validation text go hand in hand?

   c. For what purpose would you use the input mask?

   d. In what way does using the Lookup Wizard decrease the chance of entering the wrong data in a field?

3. Modifying the database is important if new information requirements arise in managing Up the Hill Bakery's business.

   a. What do you need to do to add five new customers and three new inventory items to the database?

   b. What changes do you need to make to the tables and forms if you want to add another field to the Inventory table, such as InStock?

   c. What would you need to do to the database if Jack and Susan decided to keep better track of their employees?

Dr. Garrett's Chiropractic Office
Services and Patient Database

ACCESS WORKING CASE: BEGINNING LEVEL

Submission Instructions Complete Case 2 in Access. Answer the questions at the end of this case and ask your instructor for submission instructions.

Preview You are the office manager for Dr. Garrett. She would like you to create a simple database application with two tables and two data-entry forms. This is a chiropractic office that wants to keep track of the different services and products it offers as well as patient insurance information. At the end of this case you will create two tables with various field properties and create an easy-to-use data-entry form for each table.

Skill Set

Table Design	Form Design
Field properties	Command buttons
Lookup Wizard	Calculated fields
Validation rule	Page formatting
Validation text	
Input mask	

Background Dr. Garrett owns a small chiropractic office in Tucson, Arizona. Her office provides a variety of services including different types of adjustments, massages, and herbal products. She wants to keep track of all the services and products in the office and her patients' information. She would like you to design a database application to keep her information organized.

▶ CASE ANALYSIS

Output Requirements

Dr. Garrett's chiropractic office needs a database application with a Service table and a Patient Information table and two input forms based on these tables for easy data entry and editing. You are to create this database from a blank database and save it as Dr. Garrett's Chiropractic Office.

Input Requirements

Dr. Garrett wants to create a Service table that includes information about each of her chiropractic services and products, including their unique identification number, service name, type of service or product, whether the service or product is covered by insurance, and the price of service or product, as shown in Table 2.1. She also wants to create an input form to enter information about each of her services within the Service table, including in the form all the fields mentioned above.

Similarly, Dr. Garrett wants to create a Patient Information table, which includes each of her patients' contact and insurance information, including their unique identification code, first and last name, street address, city, zip code, phone number, and the insurance provider name, as shown in Table 2.2. She wants to use an input form to enter the information about each of her patients from the Patient table.

► DESIGN AND IMPLEMENTATION

Service Table and Patient Table

Design Principle

Table 2.1 shows the layout of the Service table, where the first row contains the field names and the following rows represent a record of information for each of the chiropractic services. Table 2.2 shows the layout of the Patient table, where the first row contains the field names and the following rows represent a record of information for each of the chiropractic services.

Table 2.1 Service Table

Service Id	Service Type	Service Name	Covered by Insurance	Price Per Service or Product
S1111	Adjustment	Back alignment	Yes	$120.00
S1112	Adjustment	Neck alignment	Yes	$150.00
S1113	Adjustment	Hip alignment	Yes	$150.00
S1114	Product	Herbal energy drink	No	$42.00
S1115	Product	Vitamin C anti-wrinkle cream	No	$35.00
S1116	Product	Grape seed oil	No	$15.00
S1117	Massage	60-minute full body	No	$100.00
S1118	Massage	30-minute foot reflexology	No	$65.00
S1119	Massage	60-minute hot stone	No	$120.00

Table 2.2 Patient Table

Patient Id	First Name	Last Name	Address	City	Zip	Phone Number	Insurance Information
P1111	Susan	Wilson	2876 Del Rio	Tucson	85703	(520) 867-0987	Sharp PPO
P1112	Greg	Brown	4563 Cactus Drive	Benson	85602	(520) 657-4987	Kaiser Permanente PPO
P1113	Katie	Liversage	7654 Yucca Circle	Tucson	85705	(520) 538-5453	Blue Cross

Implementation
Service Table

1. ServiceId is a primary key. It should consist of exactly five characters: the letter A and four digits. Use validation rules and validation text to complete this step. See the Design View table in Figure 2.1.

2. The ServiceId field should have a format field property of the greater than symbol, which indicates all capital letters.

3. Select Yes for required ID for ServiceId.

4. Create a Lookup Wizard for the ServiceType field: Adjustment, Massage, Product.

5. The ServiceName field should have a field size of 40.

6. The CoveredByInsurance field is a Yes/No data type with a default answer of Yes.

7. The PricePerService/Product field should be currency with two decimal places.

8. Save the table as Service and enter the nine records as shown in Table 2.1.

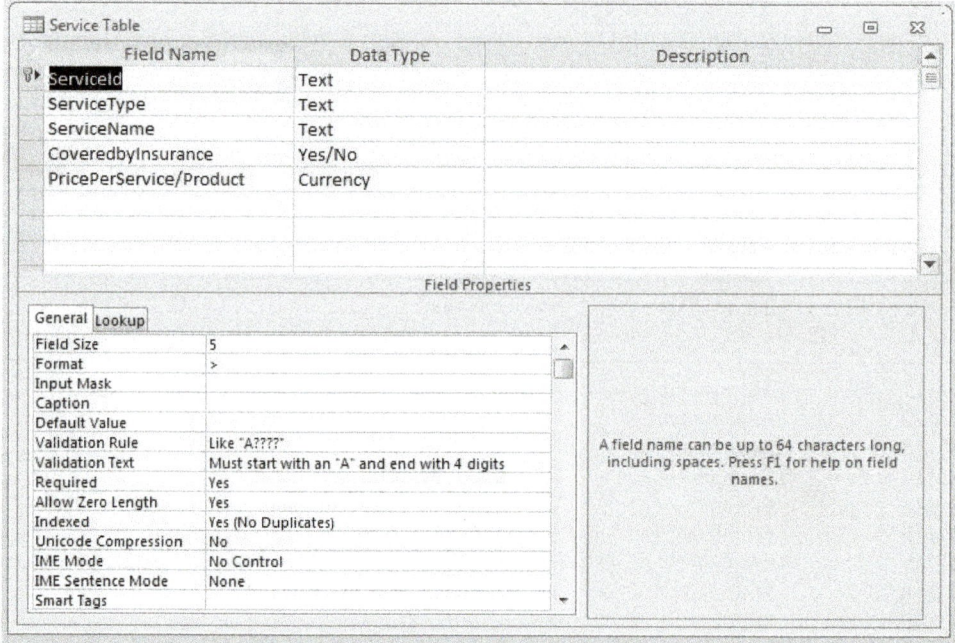

Figure 2.1   Design View of ServiceId Field Properties

Patient Table

1. PatientId is a primary key. It should only consist of exactly five characters. All patient IDs should start with a "P" for patient and end with four digits. Use validation rules and validation text to complete this step.

2. The PatientId field should have a format field property of the greater than symbol, which indicates all capital letters. PatientId is a required field.

3. The FirstName and LastName fields should have a field size of 25.
4. The Address field should have a field size of 40.
5. Create a Lookup Wizard for the City field: Tucson, Benson, Wilson, and Other.
6. The Zip code field should have a field size of 5.
7. Use the Phone Number input mask for the PhoneNumber field.
8. The Insurance information field should have a field size of 40.
9. Save the table as Patient and enter the three records as shown in Table 2.2.

Service Form and Patient Form

Design Principle
The layout of the input forms for the Service table and the Patient table are shown in Figure 2.2 and Figure 2.3.

Implementation
Service Form

1. Create a Form in Wizard from the Service table.
2. Include all fields.

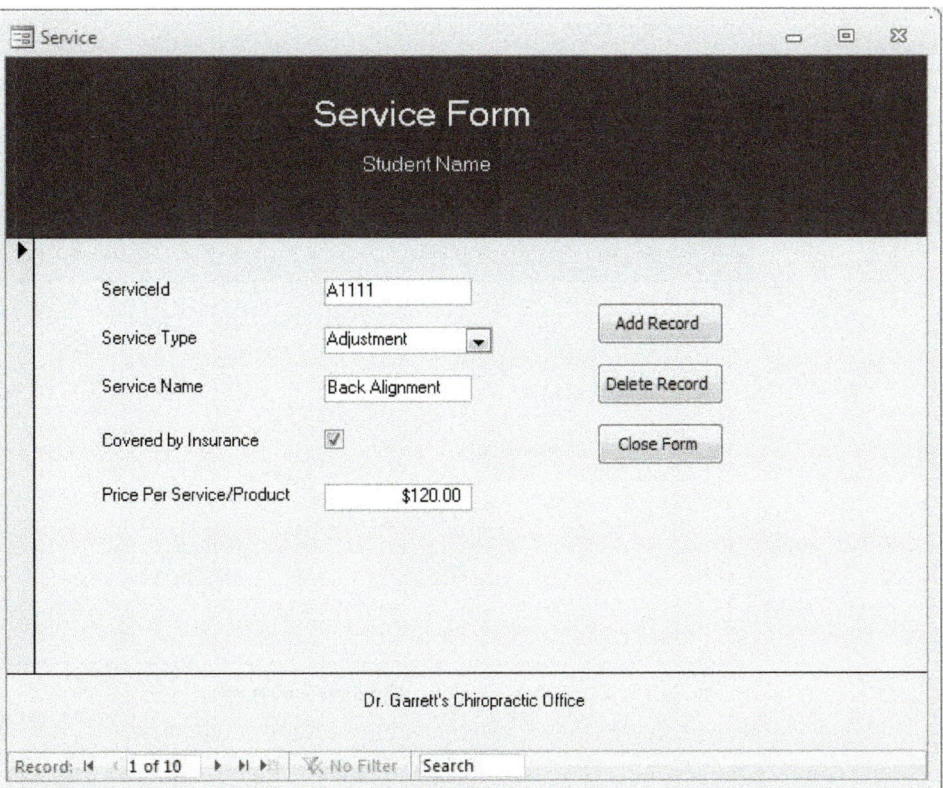

Figure 2.2 Service Input Form

3. Arrange fields as shown in Figure 2.3.
4. Include three command buttons: Add Record, Delete Record, and Close Form.
5. Include a proper form title within the header (don't forget to use the label icon!).
6. Include an additional label within the header with your first and last name.
7. Choose a different color for the Header and the Detail sections.
8. Insert a footer: Dr. Garrett's Chiropractic Office.
9. Save the form as Service Form.

Patient Form

1. Create the second form in Wizard for the Patient table.
2. Include all fields.
3. Arrange fields as shown in Figure 2.3.
4. Include three command buttons: Add Record, Delete Record, and Close Form. i.e. PatientFormAdd, PatientFormDelete, PatientFormClose.
5. Include a proper form title (don't forget to use the label icon!).
6. Include an additional label within the header with your first and last name.
7. Choose a different color for the Header and the Detail sections.
8. Insert a footer: Dr. Garrett's Chiropractic Office.
9. Save the form as Patient form.

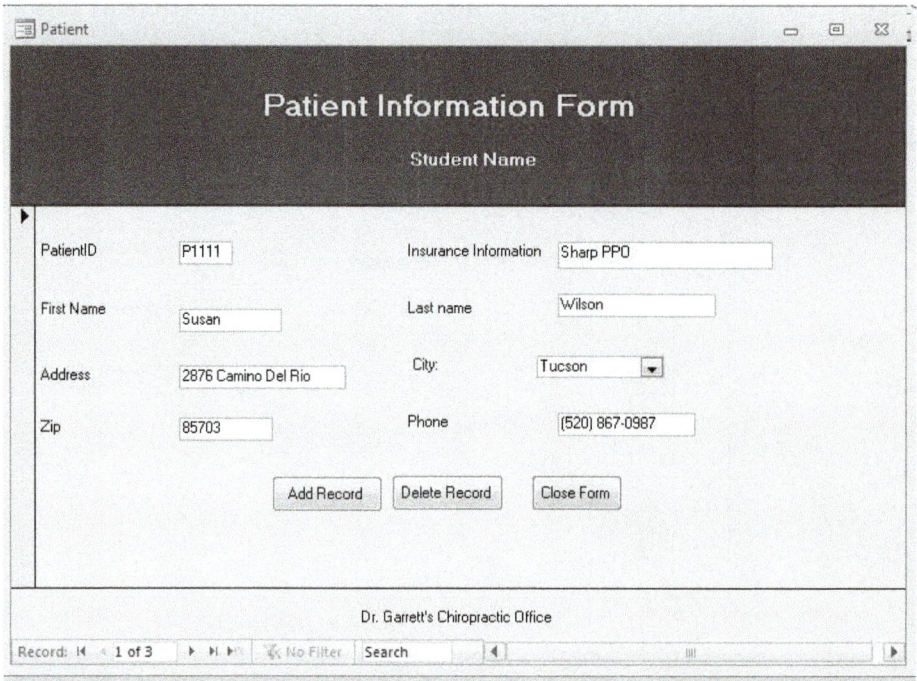

Figure 2.3 Patient Input Form

► USING THE DATABASE APPLICATION

1. Dr. Garrett's Chiropractic Office is known for its well-organized business practices, especially how it arranges its organizational information.

   a. Why are two tables—the service table and the patient table—used in the chiropractor's database? Why not just use one table?

   b. What is the purpose of each field in each of the two tables? Why is it important to specify the field properties for each field in the tables?

   c. What is the purpose of the primary key in each of the two tables? Why is it necessary to have a primary key?

2. The chiropractic office wants to make sure it has accurate service and patient information in the database.

   a. Overall, why does using the service and patient input forms increase the accuracy of information in the database?

   b. Why do the validation rule and validation text go hand in hand?

   c. For what purpose would you use the input mask?

   d. In what way does using the Lookup Wizard decrease the chance of entering the wrong data in a field?

   e. Use the Patient Input form to add yourself as a Patient to the database.

3. Modifying the database is important if new information requirements arise in managing the office's business.

   a. What do you need to do to add ten new patients and five new products to the database?

   b. Currently, Dr. Garrett provides three service types: adjustment, product, and massage. What changes would you need to make to the Service table if she added a fourth type of service, such as Acupuncture?

   c. What changes do you need to make to the tables and forms if you want to add another field to the Patient table, such as Gender?

   d. What would you need to do to the database if Dr. Garrett decided to keep better track of her patient appointments?

Home Town Realty
Real Estate Database

ACCESS WORKING CASE: BEGINNING LEVEL

Submission Instructions   Complete Case 3 in Access. Answer the questions at the end of this case and ask your instructor for submission instructions.

Preview   You are the sales manager of a real estate office and you need to create a simple database application with two tables and two data input forms. The office needs you to keep track of all property information and the selling agent's employee information. At the end of this case you will be able to create two tables with various field properties, and create an easy-to-use data-entry form for each table.

Skill Set

Table Design	Form Design
Field properties	Command buttons
Lookup Wizard	Calculated fields
Validation rule	Images and labels
Validation text	Field properties
Input mask	

Background   Home Town Realty sells real estate in California, mainly in the Orange County area. The office also provides property management services and is currently managing several apartment buildings in the area. Tom Mahoney is the owner of Home Town Realty and employs three real estate agents. He would like you, the sales manager, to design a database application for his office that includes the current property information and each agent's employee information.

▶ CASE ANALYSIS

Output Requirements

Tom Mahoney wants you, the sales manager, to create a database application with a Property table and an Employee table and two input forms based on these tables for easy data entry and editing. You are to create this database from a blank database and save it as Home Town Realty.

Input Requirements

As sales manager, you want to create a Property table to store information about each of the properties the office is currently selling or managing. New properties are listed frequently, so create an input form to enter or modify the data for each property quickly and accurately. In the Property table you need to gather information about each property, including its unique identification number, type of property, property address including city and zip, property's asking price, sale price, square footage, number of bedrooms and bathrooms, the date the property was listed and the date the property was sold, who was the listing agent, and the commission on the property. Table 3.1 shows the information for the currently listed properties. Create an input form to enter information about each of the properties, and include all the fields within the Property table.

You want to manage the real estate agent's employee information in an Employee table. You need to include a unique identification number; employee's first and last names; employee's address, city, and zip; phone number; and each agent's real estate license number and commission split with the broker, as shown in Table 3.2. You need to create an input form to be able to enter information about each of the agents. Include all the fields within the agent table.

▶ DESIGN AND IMPLEMENTATION

Property Table and Agent Table

Design Principle
Table 3.1 is the current property information for the Property table and the information for each of the six current properties. Note that there is a unique identifier code for each

Table 3.1 Information on Current Properties

Property Id	P01	P02	P03	P04
Property Type	Attach	Detach	Commercial	Multi-Unit
Property Address	1345 Juan Tabo Road	3847 Marguerite Circle	678 Dover Street	78 Bayshore Drive
Property Zip	92658	92654	92659	92658
Asking Price	$475,000	$850,000	$2,800,000	$1,200,000
Square Footage	1,700	2,200	4,000	3,000
Bedrooms	2	4	4	4
Bathrooms	1	3	3	3
Listing Date	01/13/2012	11/04/2011	10/24/2011	03/12/2012
Date Sold	04/05/2012			05/13/2012
Sales Price	$469,000			$1,038,000
Listing Agent Id	A01	A02	A02	A03
Commission from Listing	3%	2%	3%	3%

Table 3.2 Agent Information

Listing Agent Id	A01	A02	A03
First Name	Krista	William	James
Last Name	Gallegos	Wilcox	Wilson
Address	8203 Jefferson	10239 Montgomery	3894 Station Village
City	Corona Del Mar	Newport	Costa Mesa
Zip	92625	92658	92626
Phone Number	(949) 584-9472	(949) 587-0034	(949) 583-4719
License Number	R457638	R847548	R847592
Hire Date	02/01/2000	04/01/1999	05/06/2001
Commission Split with Brokerage	50%	60%	55%

of the properties. Table 3.2 is the information for the Agent table. Home Town Realty currently employs six agents. The agents each split their commission with the broker. Each commission is different depending on how long they've been with the company and what type of licenses they possess.

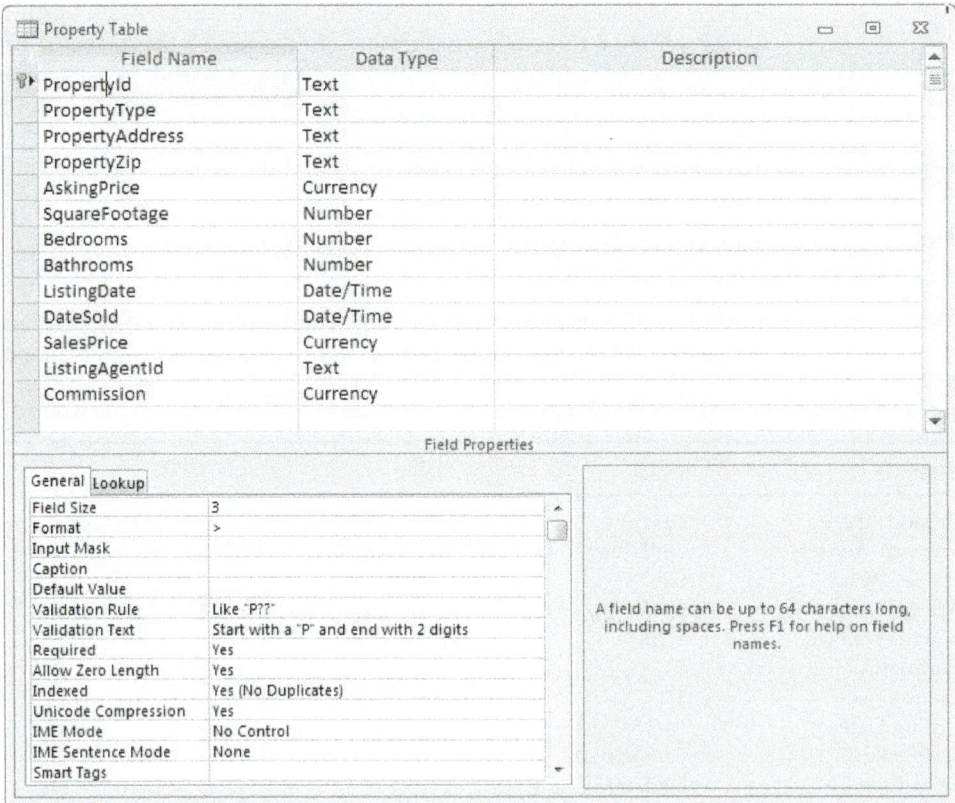

Figure 3.1 Design View of PropertyId Field Properties

Implementation
Property Table

1. PropertyId is a primary key (unique identifier code). It should consist of exactly three characters. All item IDs should start with a "P" and end with two digits. See the Design View table in Figure 3.1. Use validation rules and validation text to complete this step.

2. The PropertyId field should have a format field property of the greater than symbol, which indicates all capital letters. The PropertyId is is also a required field.

3. Create a Lookup Wizard for the PropertyType field: Attach, Detach, Commercial, Multi-Unit.

4. The PropertyAddress field size is 50.

5. Use the Zip Code input mask for the property Zip field.

6. The AskingPrice field and the SalesPrice fields are currency data type fields with no decimals.

7. The SquareFootage field is a number data type with no decimals.

8. The Bedrooms field and the Bathrooms field are number data type fields with no decimals.

9. The ListingDate field and the DateSold field are date/time data type fields with both the format property and the input mask property formatted as a short date.

10. The ListingAgentId field size is 3.

11. The Commission field is a currency data type with a format of percentage within the field properties, withno decimal places.

Agent Table

1. The ListingAgentId field is the primary key; it consists of three characters. All Listing Agent IDs should start with an "A" for agent and end with two digits. Use validation rules and validation text to complete this step.

2. The ListingAgentId field should have a format field property of the greater than symbol, which indicates all capital letters. It is a required field.

3. The AgentFirstName field and AgentLastName field should have a field size of 15.

4. Use the Zip Code input mask for the Zip code field.

5. Use the Phone Number input mask for the PhoneNumber field.

6. The LicenseNumber field should begin with the letter R followed by six digits. Use validation rules and validation text to complete this step.

7. The HireDate field is a date and time data type with a short date format.

8. The CommissionSplit field is a currency data type with the format as a percentage with zero decimals.

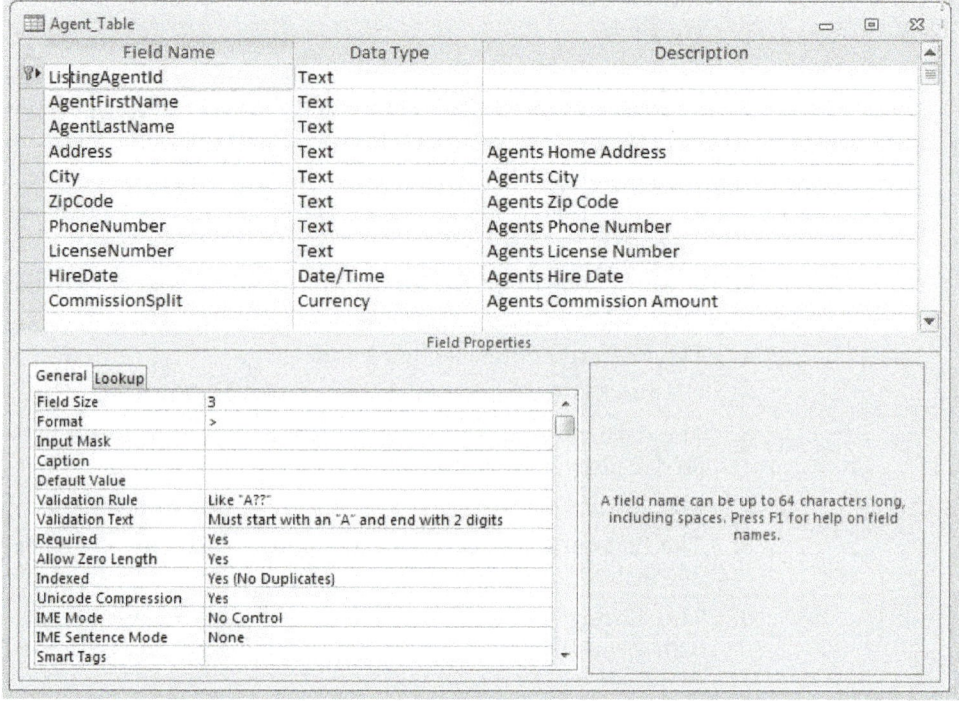

Figure 3.2 Agent Table

9. Include a description following as follows: Agent's Address for the Address Field. Insert appropriate descriptions for Agent's city, zip code, phone number, license number, hire date, and commission split. See Figure 3.2 for layout properties.

Property Form and Agent Form

Design Principle
The layout of the input forms for the Property and Agent tables are shown in Figure 3.3 and Figure 3.4.

Implementation
Property Form

1. Create a Form in Wizard from the Property table.
2. Include all fields and arrange the fields as shown in Figure 3.3.
3. Include a relevant form title (don't forget to use the label icon!).

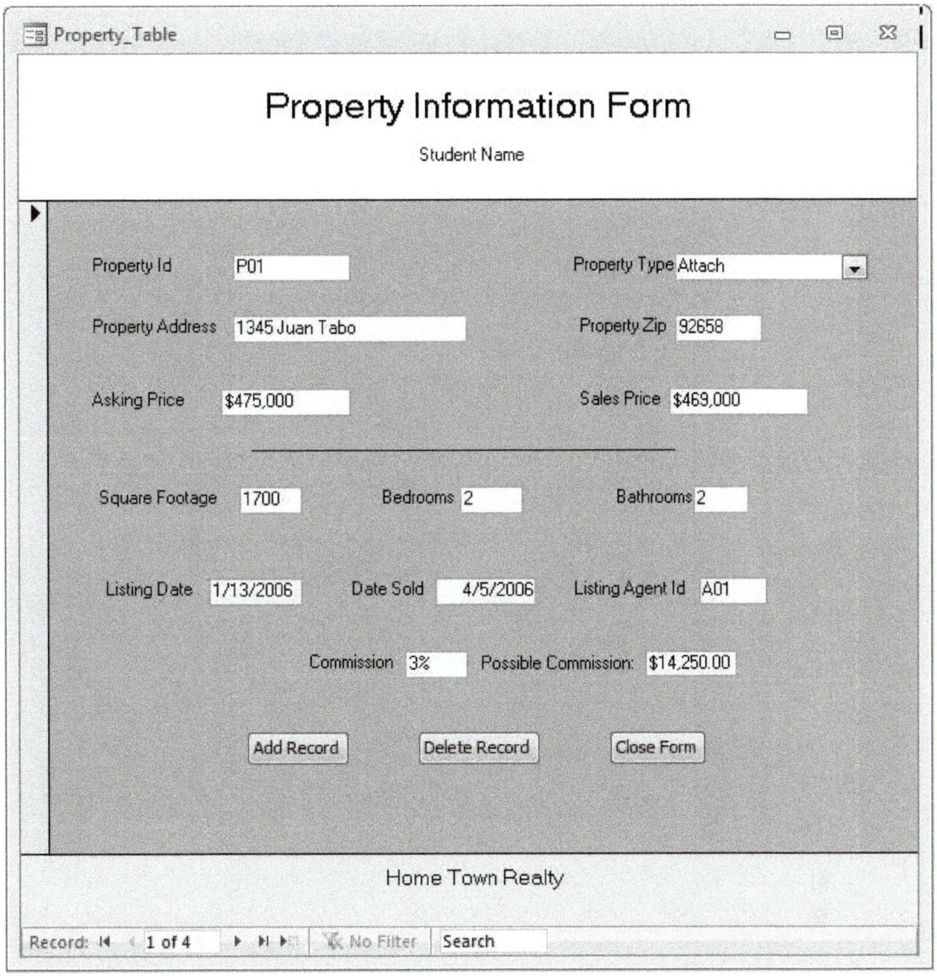

Figure 3.3 Property Form

4. Include an additional label within the header with your first and last name.

5. Include an additional label in the header with your first and last name.

6. Include a calculated field that calculates the agent's possible commission from the sale (multiply the commission rate by the asking price). Format the calculated field to show as a currency field.

7. Include three command buttons: Add Record, Delete Record, and Close Form.

8. Choose a different color for the header and the detail sections and insert a footer.

9. Save the form as Property Form.

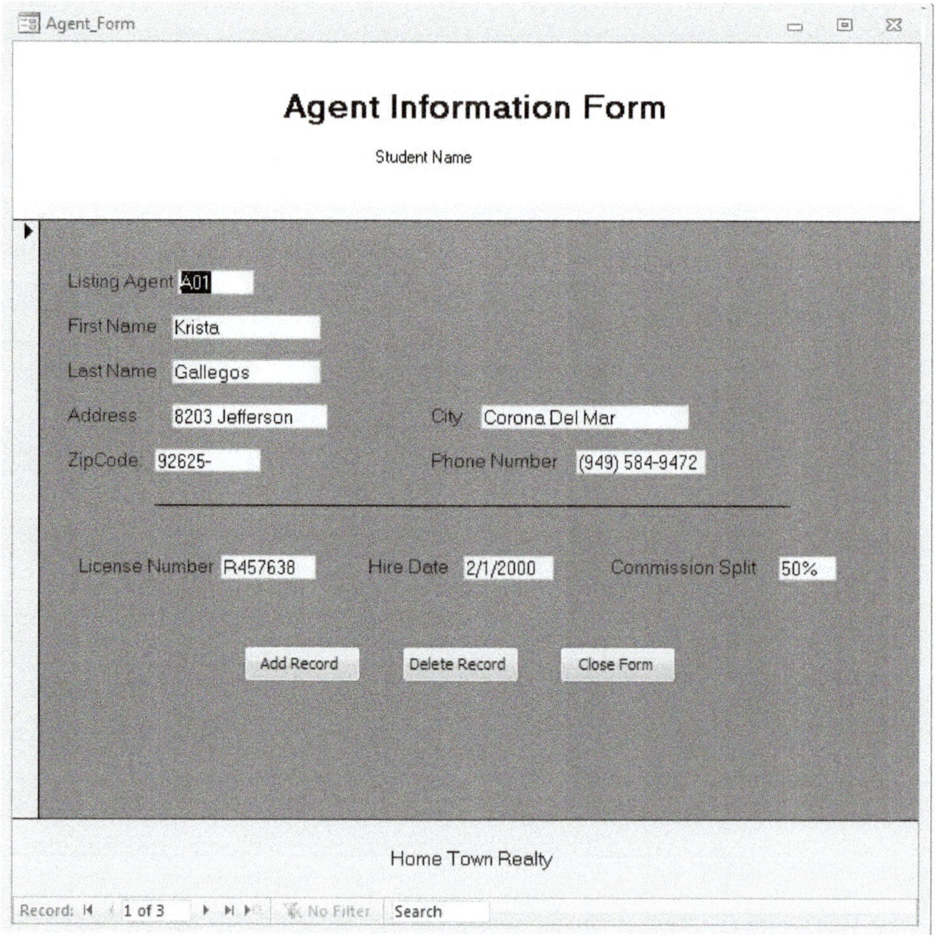

Figure 3.4 Agent Form

Agent Form

1. Create the Agent form in Wizard for the Agent table.
2. Include all fields and arrange fields as shown in Figure 3.4.
3. Include three command buttons: Add Record, Delete Record, and Close Form.
4. Include a relevant form title (don't forget to use the label icon!).
5. Include an additional label in the header with your first and last name.
6. Include clip art next to your title.
7. Choose a different color for the Header and Detail Sections. Insert a footer.
8. Save the form as Agent Form.

▷ USING THE DATABASE APPLICATION

1. In the competitive real estate industry, well-organized information in database tables is crucial for Home Town Realty.

   a. Why are two tables—the property table and the agent table—used in the Home Town Realty's database? Why not just use one table?

   b. What is the purpose of each field in each of the two tables? Why is it important to specify the field properties for each field in the tables?

   c. What is the purpose of the primary key in each of the two tables? Why is it necessary to have a primary key?

2. Entering accurate property and agent information into the database is critical for Home Town Realty.

   a. Overall, why does using the property and agent input forms increase the accuracy of information in the database?

   b. In what way does using the Lookup Wizard decrease the chance of entering the wrong data in a field?

   c. Use the Property input form to add another property record to the database. Create all the information on your own.

   d. Use the Agent input form to add a new agent to the Agent table. Create all the information on your own.

   e. Use the Agent input form to modify the phone number of one of the agents.

3. Modifying the database is important if new information requirements arise in managing Home Town Realty's business.

   a. What do you need to do to add five new properties and three new agents to the database?

   b. What changes do you need to make to the tables and forms if you want to add another field to the property table, such as parcel number?

   c. If Tom Mahoney's realty business dramatically expanded, what would you need to do to the agent table if he expects to have more than 100 agents as employees?

   d. What would you need to do if Tom Mahoney wanted to keep better track of potential customers—people who may be interested in selling or purchasing property?

CHAPTER 2

Access—Queries and Reports

Up the Hill Bakery

Inventory Control

ACCESS TEACHING CASE: INTERMEDIATE LEVEL

Submission Instructions Complete Case 4 in Access. Answer the questions at the end of this case and ask your instructor for submission instructions.

Preview You are the store manager of the bakery. You want to run several queries from the database every week to keep track of the daily and weekly business and to create reports based on these findings. From these queries you will create weekly reports and be able to build inferences based on the findings and patterns found in them. At the end of this case you will be able to create queries with a variety of selection criteria and reports based on the queries with a variety of value-added features.

Skill Set

Queries	Reports
Insert criteria	Format reports
Sorting	Sorting
Show option	Grouping
Queries based on more than one table	Header and footer
	Labels

Background As the store manager of the bakery you need to create several weekly reports showing a variety of weekly sales statistics. You need reports showing the relative popularity of the bakery items and the revenue breakdown per bakery item. As store manager you need a third weekly report providing information about the items received from outside suppliers and sold in the store; you would like to replace the suppliers whose goods are selling the least amount of inventory. You also need a report showing which bakery items are made in the store and are the least popular so you can eliminate these items and bake new ones. Finally, for a new marketing campaign you need a report listing your restaurant customers so you can send promotional information to those restaurants.

▶ CASE ANALYSIS

Output Requirements

As store manager, you need to create the queries to retrieve the information required for the reports and create five reports with an easy-to-read, attractively formatted layout.

Input Requirements

The information for the data tables has been entered for you in the database file named Case 4.

▶ DESIGN AND IMPLEMENTATION

Queries

Design Principle
A query allows you to retrieve, or select, information from any combination of fields in one or more tables based on a criterion. In Access, a query's input is the appropriate database table(s), the processing is the selection criterion represented as a logical expression, and the output is the desired fields of each of the selected records from the table(s). Figure 4.1 shows an example of a query in Design view.

Implementation
Query 1 You want to find out which inventory items are least popular so that you can possibly create a marketing campaign for those items or consider discontinuing the item. Figure 4.1 shows an example of a query in Design view.

1. In Design view, select the Inventory table as the input.
2. Include the following fields: ItemType, ItemName, and DailyAverageSold.
3. Sort DailyAverageSold in ascending order.
4. Save the query as Query 1 Least Popular Items.

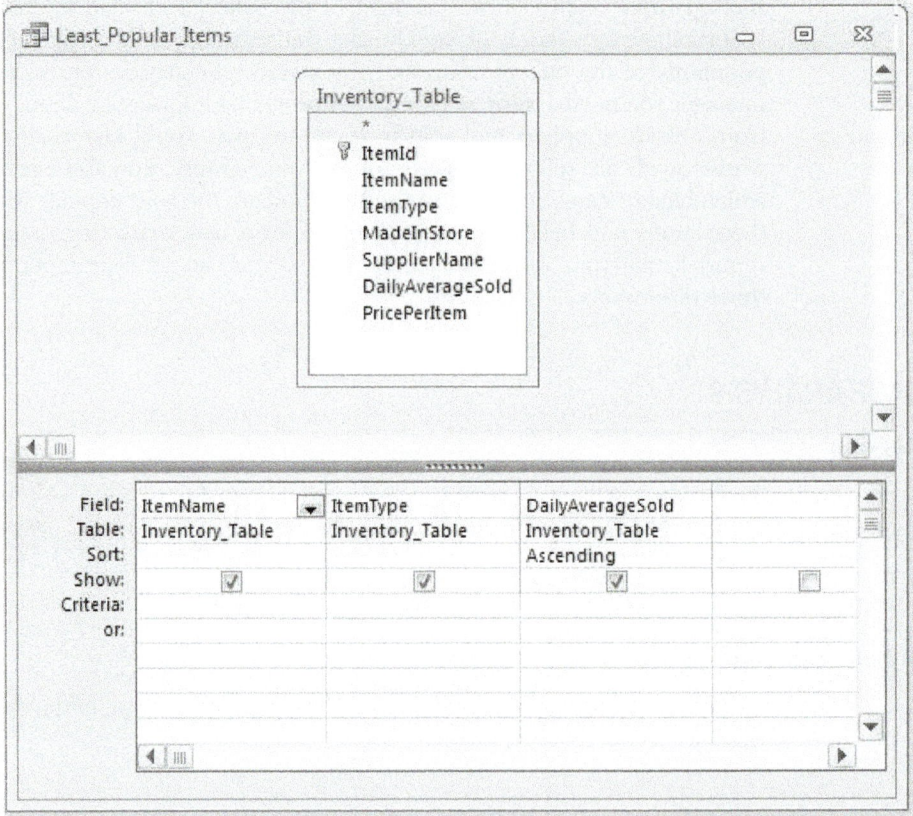

Figure 4.1   Example Query 1 in Design view

Query 2   The second query is to find out which items are yielding the most revenue per day. These items are the most popular in the bakery, and you are considering a coupon offer to attract new customers.

1.   In Design view, select the Inventory table as the input.
2.   Include the following fields: ItemType, ItemName.
3.   Create a calculated field named RevenuePerItem. The revenue calculation is

$$\text{Revenue Per Item} = [\text{DailyAverageSold}] * [\text{PricePerItem}]$$

4.   Sort Revenue Per Item in descending order.
5.   Save the query as Query 2 Revenue Per Item.

Query 3   You are always monitoring your outside supplier inventory. The bakery loses money on inventory that doesn't sell; therefore, you want to create a query to show

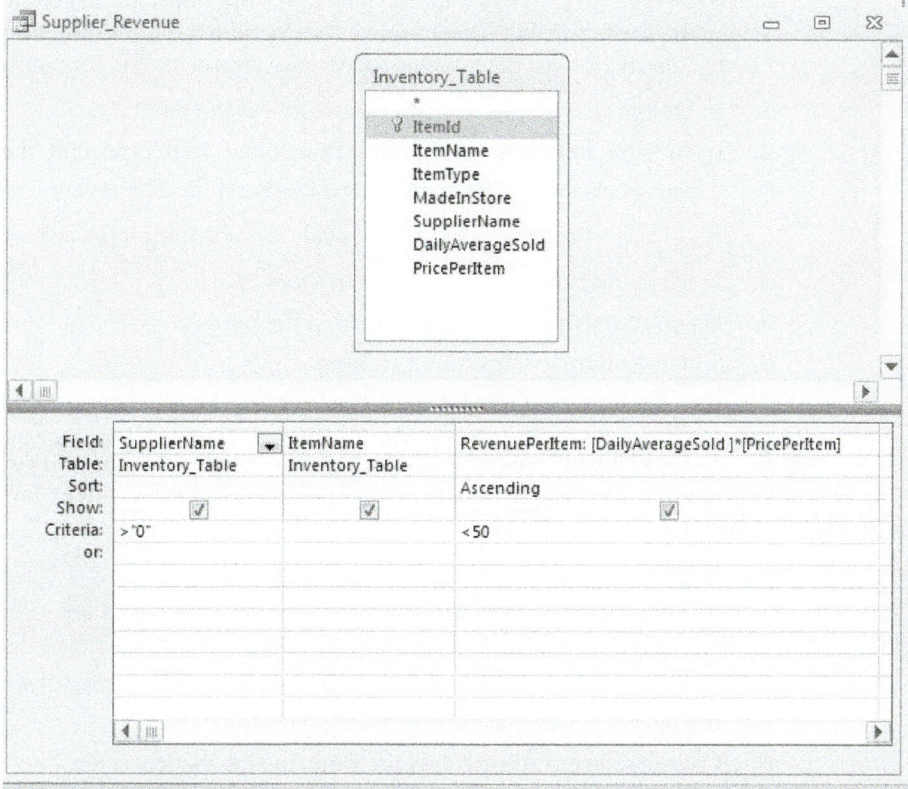

Figure 4.2 Example Query 3 in Design view

which items from your suppliers are selling the least. Figure 4.2 shows an example of a query in Design view.

1. In Design view, select the Inventory table as the input.
2. Include the following fields: SupplierName, ItemName.
3. Create a calculated field named RevenuePerItem. The revenue calculation is

$$RevenuePerItem = [DailyAverageSold] * [PricePerItem]$$

4. Sort Revenue Per Item ascending.
5. Insert a less than $50.00 criterion for RevenuePerItem.
6. Insert a greater than 0 criterion for Supplier Name (you only want to see your suppliers).
7. Save the query as Query 3 Supplier Revenue.

Query 4 You want to run a query on which store items are baked in the store and are selling the least. You will have to make the decision to either discontinue these items or create a promotion for these items to increase awareness for your customers.

1. In Design view, select the Inventory table as the input.
2. Include the following field names: ItemName, ItemType, and MadeInStore.
3. Create a calculated field named RevenuePerItem. The revenue calculation is

$$\text{RevenuePerItem} = [\text{DailyAverageSold}] * [\text{PricePerItem}]$$

4. Insert a criterion of Yes for Made in Store.
5. Do not show the MadeInStore field in the output.
6. Sort ascending for Revenue Per Item.
7. Save the query as Query 4 Baked In Store.

Query 5 You want to find out which of your customers are other restaurant owners. You need to send them a promotional package for special rates on particular bakery items.

1. In Design view, select the Customer table as the input.
2. Include the following field names: CustomerType, LastName, FirstName, Address, City, Zip.
3. Create a criterion for CustomerType and insert the criterion Restaurant.
4. Uncheck the Show criteria for CustomerType.
5. List the selected records by LastName in alphabetical order.
6. Save the query as Query 5 Restaurant Delivery Customers.

Reports

Design Principle
In Access, a report displays the retrieved information of a query in an attractive, easy-to-read format. In addition to the retrieved information, a report can have several value-added features including a title, date, footer, and groupings of records with appropriate subtotals. You can create one or more reports for a saved query.

Implementation
Report 1 Create a report based on Query 1. The report will show inventory items that are least popular. Figure 4.3 shows the report layout.

1. Create a report in Report Wizard based on Query 1 Least Popular Items.
2. Use the default layout.
3. Title the report "Least Popular Items," change the font color of the title, and center the title.
4. Create a label with your name below the title within the header.
5. Switch to Layout view and insert value-added features such as text formatting, text alignment, and color shading to increase the readability of the information.

Least Popular Items

Student Name

Item Name	Item Type	Daily Average Sold
White Chocolate Cupcake	Pastry	2
Strawberry Cream Cupcake	Pastry	4
Strawberry-Banana	Drink	5
Carrot Cupcake	Pastry	5
Spicy Olive Bread	Bread	5
Peach Peace	Drink	5
Pick Me Up Green Monster	Drink	10
Blueberry & Apricot Muffin	Pastry	12

Figure 4.3   Report 1 Layout

6. Change the date properties to short date within the footer.

7. Save the report as Report 1 Least Popular Items.

Report 2   Create a report based on Query 2. The report will list items that are yielding the most revenue per day. Figure 4.4 shows the report layout.

1. Create a report in Report Wizard based on Query 2 Revenue Per Item.

2. Wizard asks if you want to add any grouping levels. Choose by ItemType.

3. Wizard asks if you want to sort. Sort RevenuePerItem Ascending.

4. Use Summary options and select RevenuePerItem Sum.

5. Use the default layout.

6. Using the Design view, format the sum categories to show currency signs, select the sum box, and right click to choose properties and format it as currency. Apply the same formatting to the grand total.

7. Change the font color for the sum.

8. Title the report "Daily Revenue" and center the title.

9. Create a label with your name below the title within the header.

10. Switch to Layout view and insert value-added features such as text formatting, text alignment, and color shading to increase the readability of the information.

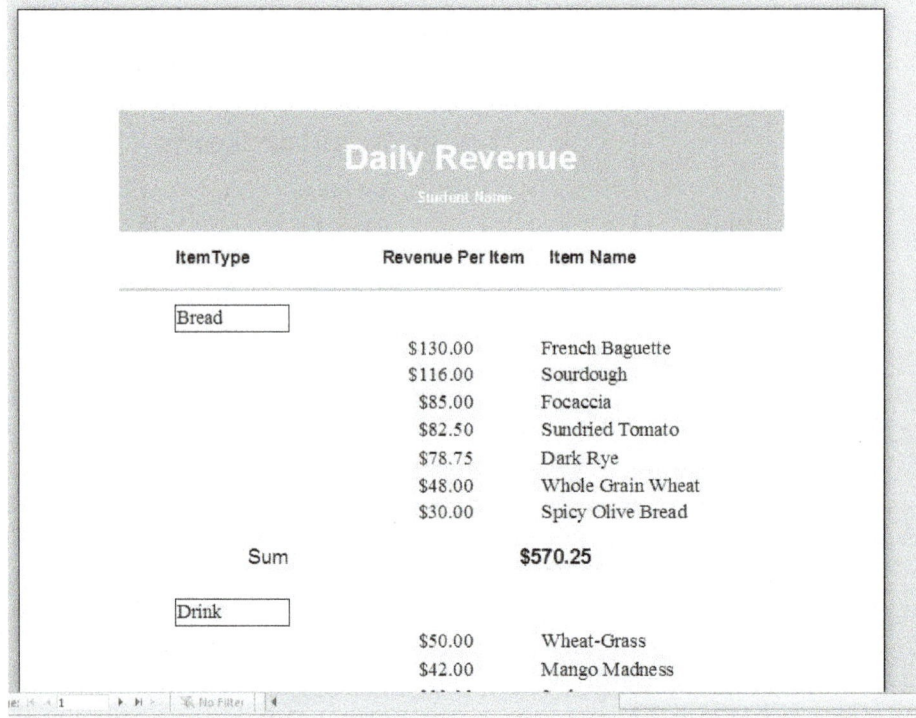

Figure 4.4 Report 2 Layout

11. Change the date properties to short date within the footer.
12. Save the report as Report 2 Revenue Per Item.

Report 3 Create a report based on Query 3. The report will list items that come from outside suppliers and that are selling the least.

1. Create a report in Report Wizard based on Query 3 Supplier Revenue.
2. Group by Supplier Name.
3. Wizard asks if you want to sort. Sort RevenuePerItem Ascending.
4. Use Summary options and select RevenuePerItem Sum.
5. In the Summary options, select the radio button Summary Only.
6. Use the default layout.
7. Using the Design view, format the sum categories to show currency signs, select the sum box, and right click to choose properties and format it as currency.
8. Title the report "Daily Supplier Revenue" and center the title.
9. Create a label with your name below the title within the header.

10. Switch to Layout view and insert value-added features such as text formatting, text alignment, and color shading to increase the readability of the information.

11. Change the date properties to short date within the footer.

12. Save the report as Report 3 Supplier Revenue.

Report 4 Create a report based on Query 4. The report will list bakery items that are baked in the store and are selling the least.

1. Create a report in Report Wizard based on Query 4 Baked In Store.

2. Add a grouping level by ItemType.

3. Sort ascending by RevenuePerItem.

4. Use the default layout.

5. Title the report "Baked In Store" and center the title.

6. Create a label with your name below the title within the header.

7. Switch to Layout view and insert value-added features such as text formatting, text alignment, and color shading to increase the readability of the information.

8. Change the date properties to short date and center the date within the footer.

9. Save the report as Report 4 Baked In Store.

Report 5 Create a report based on Query 5. The report will show which of your customers are other restaurant owners.

1. Create a report in Report Wizard based on Query 5 Restaurant Delivery Customers.

2. Use the default layout.

3. Title the report "Restaurant Delivery Customers," change the font color of the title, and center the title.

4. Create a label with your name below the title within the header.

5. Switch to Layout view and insert value-added features such as text formatting, text alignment, and color shading to increase the readability of the information.

6. Change the date properties to short date within the footer.

7. Save the report as Report 5 Restaurant Delivery Customers.

► USING THE APPLICATION

1. As the bakery's store manager, you conduct the weekly evaluation of the business by reviewing the various reports.

   a. Refer to Report 1 Least Popular Items and name the top three inventory items that are least popular.

   b. Refer to Report 2 Revenue per Item. Which top two individual items are yielding the most profit within each item type? What is the grand total revenue of all items sold?

    c. Refer to Report 3 Supplier Revenue. Are there any items you need to discontinue?

    d. Refer to Report 4 Baked in Store. Which store items in each group are selling the least? Which store items created in the store are yielding the most revenue?

    e. Refer to Report 5 Restaurant Delivery Customers. How many delivery customers are restaurant customers?

2. You are thinking of changing some of the reports to help improve your weekly review process.

    a. How would you modify Query 1 so you can visually scan Report 1 quickly for the top-selling inventory items?

    b. Query 2 calculates the week's revenue per item. How would you modify Query 2 to show in Report 2 also a calculated forecast of the revenue per item for the next two weeks?

    c. How would you modify Query 3 so you can see in Report 3 both the poor-selling items, those with revenues less than $50, and the most popular items, those with revenues more than $100?

    d. How would you modify Query 5 to show in Report 5 the restaurant customers in a particular zip code?

Earth Foods Grocery Store
Special Services Database
ACCESS WORKING CASE: INTERMEDIATE LEVEL

Submission Instructions   Complete Case 5 in Access. Answer the questions at the end of this case and ask your instructor for submission instructions.

Preview   You are the regional manager for special services at Earth Foods grocery stores located in New Mexico. You manage the additional services section that is provided in the grocery store. These special services include banking, floral service, coffee shop, and others. As regional manager you need to create various queries and reports to supervise the different services within the grocery store.

Skill Set

Queries	Reports
Insert criteria	Format reports
Sorting	Sorting
Show option	Grouping
Queries based on more than	Header and footer
one table	Labels

Background   Earth Foods is a major chain of 12 grocery stores throughout the state of New Mexico. In addition to selling groceries, many of the stores provide unique services to meet their customers' needs; these services include in-store dry-cleaning, banking, floral service, coffee shop, post office, and others. Not all the grocery stores have these extra services. Earth Foods has created a prototype set of database tables but has not developed a way of retrieving and reporting which stores have the different type of services and who manages them. You are to create the queries and the reports that are needed to manage these extra services appropriately.

▶ CASE ANALYSIS

Output Requirements

As regional manager you need to create multiple queries to retrieve the information required for five reports and to design those reports with an easy-to-read, attractively formatted layout.

Input Requirements

Earth Foods has developed three tables that provide information about the in-store services, the managers, and the grocery stores' contact information. The InStoreServices table, the ManagersInfo table, and the StoreAddress table are in the Case 5 database.

▶ DESIGN AND IMPLEMENTATION

Queries

Design Principle

An advantage of a relational database is that a user can retrieve information from more than one table in the database to answer a question. In Access, a query's input is the appropriate database table(s), the processing is the selection criterion represented as a logical expression, and the output is the desired fields of each of the selected records from the table(s).

Implementation

Open the Access file titled Case 5, and examine each of the three tables. Note the field names and attribute information in each table; note also the unique code—the primary key field—used for each store and each manager. Select the Relationships tool and note how the three tables are related based on the StoreID and ManagerID fields

Query 1   You want to create and send a survey to the customers who purchase flowers from the floral department in the grocery store, but you first want to run a query to find out which grocery stores in the area have floral services. Figure 5.1 shows an example of a query in Design view.

1. In Design view, select the StoreAddress table and InStoreServices table as the input.
2. Include the following fields in the query: StoreLocation, StoreAddress, StorePhoneNumber, ManagerID, and Floral.
3. Select the stores that have floral services as the criterion.
4. Do not show the Floral field in the output.
5. Sort the output list by Store Location in alphabetical order.
6. Save the query as Query1 Floral Services.

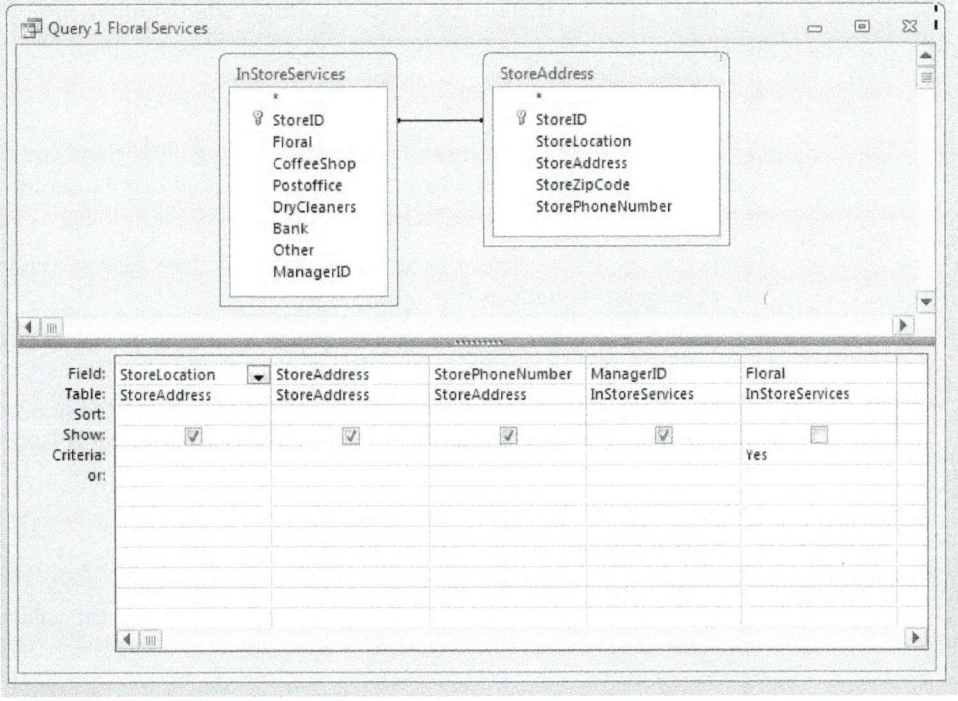

Figure 5.1 Example Query 1 in Design view

Query 2 The purpose for other services provided in the grocery store is to serve as a test market for new services you can offer in the grocery stores. You want to find out which stores have other services so you can further research their profitability.

1. In Design view, select the StoreAddress table and the InStoreServices table as the input.
2. Include the following fields in the query: StoreLocation, StorePhoneNumber, and Other.
3. Select the stores that only have other services. (Hint: Criterion is >0.)
4. Sort the output list by StoreLocation in alphabetical order.
5. Save the query as Query2 Other Services.

Query 3 You need to update the content for the grocery store's website and want to find out which stores have a deli service only.

1. In Design view, select the Queries tab instead of the Tables tab and then add the Query 2 Other Services query as the input.

2. Insert all three fields: StoreLocation, StorePhoneNumber, Other.

3. Design a criterion to find the stores that only have a deli service.

4. Save the query as Query 3 Deli Services.

Query 4   Your Albuquerque coffee carts are very profitable and you want to expand the coffee cart service to other stores that are not located in Albuquerque. Run a query to find out which stores in New Mexico but not in Albuquerque have coffee carts.

1. In Design view, select the StoreAddress table, the InStoreServices table, and the ManagersInfo table as the input.

2. Include the following fields in the query: ManagerLastName, ManagerFirstName, StoreLocation, StorePhoneNumber, and CoffeeShop.

3. Select the stores that have coffee shops and are not located in Albuquerque. (Hints: The two criteria are typed on the same criteria row; the StoreLocation criterion uses the phrase NOT.)

4. Do not show the CoffeeShop field in the output.

5. Save the query as Query 4 Coffee Shop.

Query 5   To keep up with inflation you want to increase the salary of some of your managers. You need to find out which managers were hired before 07/01/2008 and earn less than $30,000.

1. In Design view, select the ManagersInfo table as the input.

2. Insert the fields ManagerFirstName, ManagerLastName, ManagerHireDate, ManagerSalary.

3. As the criteria, show the managers who have a hire date before July 1, 2008, and who have a salary less than $30,000.

4. Sort the output list by the earliest hire date first.

5. Save the query as Query 5 Manager Salary Increase.

Reports

Design Principle
In Access, a report displays the output of a query in an easy-to-read layout. A report is especially useful to show the output of a total query, grouping the summary information by category.

Implementation
Report 1   Create a report that shows which grocery stores in the area have a floral service. Figure 5.2 shows the report layout.

1. Create a report in Report Wizard based on Query 1 Floral Services.

2. Use the default layout.

3. Title the report "Stores with Floral Service."

Stores Floral Services

Student Name

Store Location	Store Address	Store Phone Number	ManagerID
Albuquerque	456 Wyoming	(505) 675-4343	M234
Santa Fe	Main St.	(505) 878-9854	M233
Santa Fe	845 Franklin Ave	(505) 465-7678	M233
Silver City	432 Bullard Ave	(506) 943-4521	M232
Las Cruces	89 Washington Ave	(505) 934-2214	M235
TorC	90 Whistle Cir.	(505) 887-6655	M236

Figure 5.2 Report 1 Layout

4. Change the font style and font color of the title.
5. Create a label with your name below the title within the header.
6. Switch to Layout view and insert value-added features such as text formatting, text alignment, and color shading to increase the readability of the information.
7. Change the date properties to short date within the footer.
8. Save the report as Report 1 Floral Services.

Report 2 Create a report to show which stores have other services.

1. Create a report in Report Wizard based on Query 2 Other Services.
2. Use the default layout.
3. Title the report "Stores with Other Services."
4. Change the font style and font color of the title.
5. Create a label with your name below the title within the header.
6. Switch to Layout view and insert value-added features such as text formatting, text alignment, and color shading to increase the readability of the information.

7. Change the date properties to short date within the footer.
8. Save the report as Report 2 Other Services.

Report 3   Create a report to show which stores have a deli service only.

1. Create a report in Report Wizard based on Query 3 Deli Services.
2. Use the default layout.
3. Title the report "Stores with a Deli."
4. Change the font style and font color of the title.
5. Create a label with your name below the title within the header.
6. Switch to Layout view and insert value-added features such as text formatting, text alignment, and color shading to increase the readability of the information.
7. Change the date properties to short date within the footer.
8. Save the report as Report 3 Deli Services.

Report 4   Create a report to show which stores that have coffee carts are not in Albuquerque.

1. Create a report in Report Wizard based on Query 4 Coffee Shop.
2. Use the default layout.
3. Title the report "Stores with Coffee Shops excluding Albuquerque."
4. Change the font style and font color of the title.
5. Create a label with your name below the title within the header.
6. Switch to Layout view and insert value-added features such as text formatting, text alignment, and color shading to increase the readability of the information.
7. Change the date properties to short date within the footer.
8. Save the report as Report 4 Coffee Shop.

Report 5   Create a report to show which managers were hired before 07/01/2008 and earn less than $30,000.

1. Create a report in Report Wizard based on Query 5 Manager Salary Increase.
2. Use the default layout.
3. Title the report "Managers Inflation Salary Increase."
4. Change the font color of the title.
5. Create a label with your name below the title within the header.
6. Switch to Layout view and insert value-added features such as text formatting, text alignment, and color shading to increase the readability of the information.
7. Change the date properties to short date within the footer.
8. Save the report as Report 5 Manager Salary Increase.

► USING THE DATABASE APPLICATION

1. As the New Mexico regional manager, you want to have the flexibility to modify the various queries and reports as needed.

    a. Modify the Query 1 Floral Services query to select stores in Santa Fe that have a floral service. Use Report 1 Floral Services to view the new query result. Do you need to modify the Report 1 layout?

    b. Modify Query 2 Other Services to include each selected store's address and zip code. Modify Report 2 Other Services to include these new fields.

    c. Modify Query 4 Coffee Shop to select stores with coffee shops in Las Cruces and in Santa Fe. Use Report 4 Coffee Shop to view the new query result.

2. New reporting requirements arise from time to time.

    a. Design a query and report to show the managers and stores that have floral services. Save the query and report as Managers at Stores with Floral Services.

    b. Describe how you would modify the InStoreServices table to save prior year annual sales of each of the in-store services: dry cleaning, banking, floral service, coffee shop, and post office. Describe how would you design a report based on the revised InStoreServices table to show the total prior year annual sales for each of the stores.

Destination Corporate Event Planning, Inc.

Event Coordinator

ACCESS WORKING CASE: INTERMEDIATE LEVEL

Submission Instructions   Complete Case 6 in Access. Answer the questions at the end of this case and ask your instructor for submission instructions.

Preview   You are an event coordinator for a corporate event planning company, and your objective is to build several criteria-based queries and reports based on information found in the Destination Corporate Event Planning (DCP) database. DCP needs you to generate reports for current event scheduling and billing to their accounts.

Skill Set

Queries	Reports
Insert criteria	Format reports
Sorting	Sorting
Show option	Grouping
Queries based on more than one table	Header and footer
	Labels

Background   DCP is a corporate event planning company that only carries large national accounts. The company coordinates events including annual sales meetings and large conventions. Attendance at these events is a minimum of 1,000 people up to 15,000 people. At any given time DCP coordinates up to five events simultaneously. DCP uses many database files within its company, including client information and supplier and vendor information. DCP needs you to design a small part of their database just to keep track of the event dates and booking fees to the events. As an event coordinator you need to be able to run queries and reports based on the scheduling of the events as well as the cost and profit of the event.

▶ CASE ANALYSIS

Output Requirements

DCP wants you to create five reports based on five queries to retrieve information from their database.

Input Requirements

DCP has developed three tables in their database to store information about three important entities in its business: clients, suppliers, and events. The ClientInformation table, the SupplierInformation table, and the EventSchedule table are in the Case 6 database.

▶ DESIGN AND IMPLEMENTATION

Queries

Design Principle

A query allows you to select information from several related tables based on search criteria and then perform summary statistics and database processing tasks with the retrieved information.

Implementation

Open the Access file titled Case 6, and examine each of the three tables. Note the field names and attribute information in each table. Note also the unique code, otherwise known as the primary key field, used in each of the tables. Select the Relationships tool and note how the ClientInformation table and the EventSchedule table are related based on the ClientID field.

Query 1 You are running a special marketing campaign that is just focused on your California clients. You need to create a query listing California clients only. Figure 6.1 shows an example of a query in Design view.

1. In Design view, select the ClientInformation table as the input.
2. Include the following fields in the query: ClientName, ClientContactName, Client-PhoneNumber, and ClientState.
3. Design the criterion to filter only DCP's clients in California.
4. Sort the output list by ClientName in alphabetical order.
5. Save the query as Query 1 California Clients.

Query 2 When you are planning an event you want to use the suppliers in your database who have the most experience and highest rating. Create a query listing your most-experienced, highest-rated suppliers.

1. In Design view, select the SupplierInformation table as the input.
2. Include the following fields in the query: SupplierName, SupplierType, Supplier-Rating, Discount, and EventStartDate.

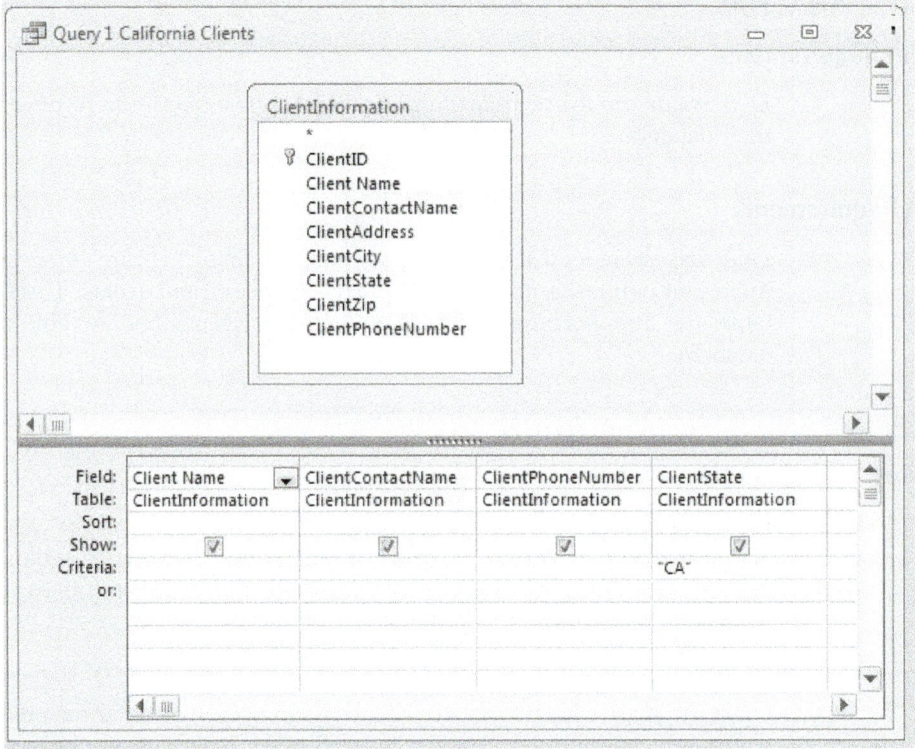

Figure 6.1 Example Query 1 in Design view

3. Design the criterion to filter the suppliers that have equal to or greater than a 4-star rating and started working with DCP after January 1, 2000.

4. Sort the output list by SupplierRating in descending order.

5. Save the query as Query 2 Experienced Suppliers.

Query 3   Each event is assigned a supervisor who is required to be on call for that event in case of an emergency. Create a query for the length (in days) for each event DCP is currently coordinating.

1. In Design view, select the ClientInformation table and the EventSchedule table as the input.

2. Include the following fields in the query: EventName, ClientName, and Number-Attending.

3. Create also in the query a calculated field named DaysOfEvent that counts how many days each event runs. (Hint: You need to subtract the EventStopDate from the EventStartDate.)

4. Sort the output list by DaysOfEvent in ascending order.

5. Save the query as Query 3 Event Length.

Query 4 Create a query that will show the profit for each event DSP has coordinated.

1. In Design view, select the EventSchedule table and the ClientInformation table as the input.
2. Include the following fields in the query: EventName, ClientName, EventTotalCost, and EventTotalPrice.
3. Create a calculated field named TotalProfit that calculates the total profit for each event. (Hint: You need to subtract EventTotalCost from EventTotalPrice.)
4. Format the TotalProfit field as currency.
5. Sort the output list by TotalProfit in descending order.
6. Save the query as Query 4 Event Profit.

Query 5 To make sure an event is profitable, you need a breakdown by cost per person. This allows you to better coordinate your events in the future. What is the cost per person for each event?

1. In Design view, select the EventSchedule table and the ClientInformation table as the input.
2. Include the following fields in the query: EventName, ClientName, and Number-Attending.
3. Create a calculated field named CostPerPerson that calculates what it costs per person for each event. (Hint: You need to divide the NumberAttending by Event-TotalCost.)
4. Format the CostPerPerson field as currency.
5. Format the NumberAttending field as a number with no decimals.
6. Sort the output list by CostPerPerson in descending order.
7. Save the query as Query 5 Event Cost Per Person.

Reports

Design Principle
In Access, a report displays the output of a query in an easy-to-read layout. A report is especially useful to show the output of a total query, grouping the summary information by category.

Implementation
Report 1 Create a report that lists California clients only. Figure 6.2 shows the report layout.

1. Create a report in Report Wizard based on Query 1 California Clients.
2. Select all available fields.
3. Use the default layout.
4. Title the report "Clients in California."
5. Change the font color and font style of the title.
6. Create a label with your name and course number below the title within the header.

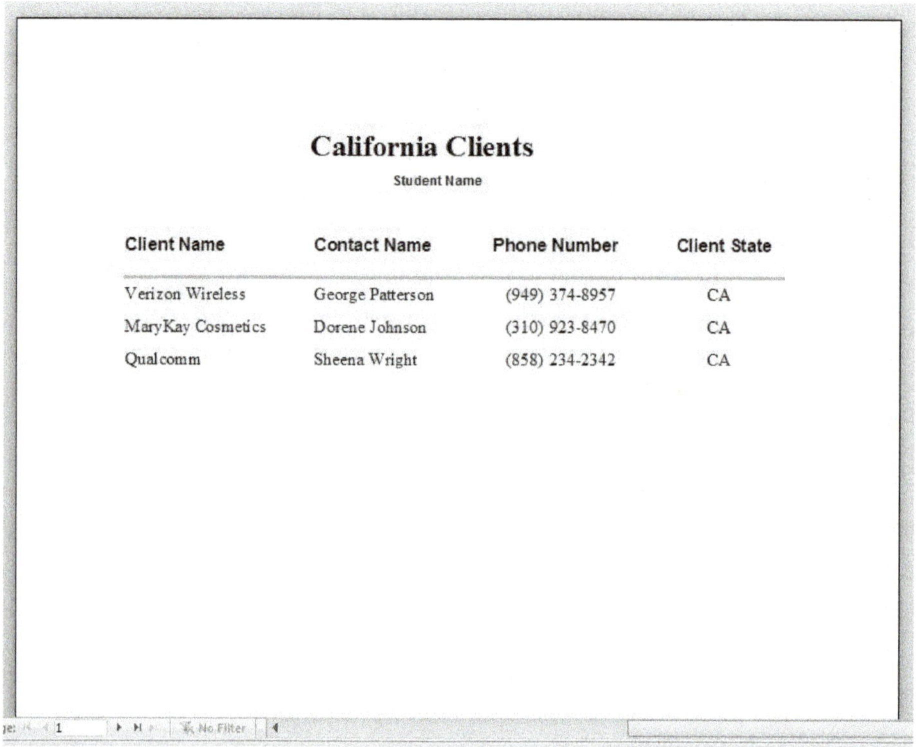

California Clients
Student Name

Client Name	Contact Name	Phone Number	Client State
Verizon Wireless	George Patterson	(949) 374-8957	CA
MaryKay Cosmetics	Dorene Johnson	(310) 923-8470	CA
Qualcomm	Sheena Wright	(858) 234-2342	CA

ie: ⏮ ◀ 1 ▶ ▶ ⏭ 🏷 No Filter ◀

Figure 6.2 Report 1 Layout

7. Switch to Layout view and insert value-added features such as text formatting, text alignment, and color shading to increase the readability of the information.
8. Change the date properties to short date within the footer.
9. Save the report as Report 1 California Clients.

Report 2   Create a report that lists your most-experienced, highest-performing suppliers.

1. Create a report in Report Wizard based on the Query 2 Experienced Suppliers.
2. Select all available fields.
3. Use the default layout.
4. Title the report "Suppliers with a 4-Star Rating and Higher."
5. Change the font color and font style of the title.
6. Create a label with your name and course number below the title within the header.
7. Switch to Layout view and insert value-added features such as text formatting, text alignment, and color shading to increase the readability of the information.
8. Change the date properties to short date within the footer.
9. Save the report as Report 2 Experienced Suppliers.

Report 3   Create a report for the on-call person for each event.

1. Create a report in Report Wizard based on Query 3 Event Length.
2. Select all available fields.
3. Use the default layout.
4. Title the report "Number of Days Per Event."
5. Change the font color and font style of the title.
6. Create a label with your name and course number below the title within the header.
7. Switch to Layout view and insert value-added features such as text formatting, text alignment, and color shading to increase the readability of the information.
8. Change the date properties to short date within the footer.
9. Save the report as Report 3 Event Length.

Report 4   Create a report that shows the profit for each event DCP has coordinated.

1. Create a report in Report Wizard based on Query 4 Event Profit.
2. Select all available fields.
3. Use the default layout.
4. Title the report "Event Profit."
5. Change the font color and font style of the title.
6. Create a label with your name and course number below the title within the header.
7. Switch to Layout view and insert value-added features such as text formatting, text alignment, and color shading to increase the readability of the information.
8. Change the date properties to short date within the footer.
9. Save the report as Report 4 Event Profit.

Report 5   Create a report to list the cost per person for each event.

1. Create a report in Report Wizard based on Query 5 Event Cost Per Person.
2. Select all available fields.
3. Use landscape as the page layout.
4. Use the default layout.
5. Title the report "Cost Per Person."
6. Change the font color and font style of the title.
7. Create a label with your name and course number below the title within the header.
8. Switch to Layout view and insert value-added features such as text formatting, text alignment, and color shading to increase the readability of the information.
9. Change the date properties to short date within the footer.
10. Save the report as Report 5 Event Cost Per Person.

▶ USING THE DATABASE APPLICATION

1. As the event coordinator, you need to revise your queries as the situations change.

   a. Modify Query 1 California Clients to show the event name associated with the California clients. (Hint: You need to include the EventSchedule table in the query.)

   b. Modify Query 2 Experienced Suppliers to include each supplier's address. Modify the Experienced Suppliers report to show this new field.

   c. Modify Query 3 Event Length to select events of more than three days. Use the Event Length report to view the new query result.

   d. Modify the Query 4 Event Profit query to select events with a profit greater than $50,000. Use the Event Profit report to view the new query result.

2. As the event coordinator, you are constantly responding to new information requirements.

   a. Design a query and report to show relevant event and client information about events with more than 2,000 people attending.

   b. If you were to create a new table to show the various suppliers for a particular event what fields would you include within the new table in order to create relationships with the EventSchedule table and the SupplierInformation table?

CHAPTER 3

Access—Advanced Queries and Reports

Up the Hill Bakery
Customer Order Database

ACCESS TEACHING CASE: ADVANCED LEVEL

Submission Instructions Complete Case 7 in Access. Answer the questions at the end of this case and ask your instructor for submission instructions.

Preview You are the manager of the Up the Hill Bakery and you need to keep track of the daily delivery orders by customers. At the end of the day you need to run a report on how many bakery items the chefs need to bake for the next morning delivery. You also need to create a daily report of the billing amount for each of the delivery orders.

Skill Set

One-to-many table relationship
Parameter query
Grouping query
Make-Table query
Delete-Table query

Background   As the manager of the small bakery, you want to keep track of product and customer information in two database tables. The bakery provides a delivery service for fresh bread and pastries to local residents, offices, and small restaurants. The chefs need a daily report of how many bakery items they need to bake for delivery and you need a daily report of the billing amount for each of the delivery orders. In addition, you want to make a few changes to the customer table, and create a new database table for restaurants only, which involves deleting the restaurant information from the existing customer table.

▶ CASE ANALYSIS

Output Requirements

Edit the Order table and create five new queries and three new reports. Create a new table by using the Make-Table query, and use the Delete query to delete fields from the existing Customer table.

Input Requirements

Table 7.1 shows information that needs to be added to the Order table.

▶ DESIGN AND IMPLEMENTATION

Order Table and Database Table Relationships

Design Principle

Table 7.1 shows the information three new items for a particular delivery order. You need to input these three items in into the Order table. Note that an order has a unique order code, and because an order can comprise several different bakery items, a record is created for each bakery item in the order. The primary key is the OrderID field. The CustomerID and ItemID fields are the primary key fields in the Customer and Inventory tables, respectively; this allows the three tables to be linked, or related, so that information from the tables can be retrieved easily. In the Up the Hill Bakery database, one customer can have several orders (a one-to-many relationship), and one bakery item can be on several orders (a one-to-many relationship).

Implementation

1.   Open the Access file titled Case 7.
2.   Open the Order table and note its structure and content, then close the Order table.

Table 7.1   Order table

OrderId	CustomerID	ItemId	Quantity	DeliveryDate
R116	C124	B411	8	06/01/2013
R116	C124	B421	6	06/01/2013
R116	C124	B531	12	06/01/2013

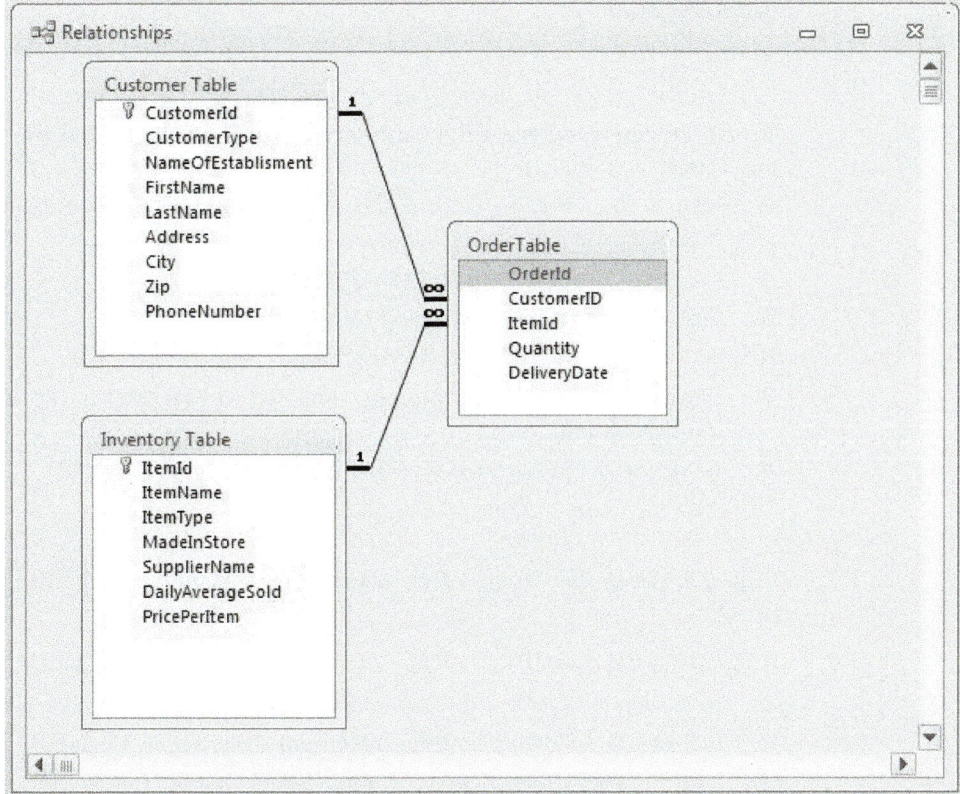

Figure 7.1   One-to-Many Relationship

3.   Open the Order table and enter the new information shown in Table 7.1.
4.   Use the Relationships tool to create a one-to-many relationship with referential integrity between the Inventory table and Order table, and between the Customer table and Order table, as shown in Figure 7.1.

Queries

Design Principle

A query allows you to retrieve, or select, information from several related tables based on search criteria. There are several variations on the design of a selected query. You can design the query to ask, or prompt, the user to enter the criteria value, referred to as a Parameter query. Another variation is a Total query that performs a desired arithmetic calculation on a group of records. A Make-Table query can also be used to create a new table with the information retrieved from one or more related tables. A Delete query can be used to delete information from a table based on a criterion.

Implementation

Query 1: Parameter Query   Which customers are requesting a certain bakery item?

1. On the Create tab, in the Query group, click on Query Design.
2. In Design view, select the Customer table, Order table, and Inventory table as the input.
3. Include the following fields in the output from the Customer table: CustomerType, NameOfEstablishment, FirstName, PhoneNumber.
4. From the Order table insert the Quantity field.
5. From the Inventory table insert the ItemId field.
6. Sort CustomerFirstName alphabetically.
7. Enter text Item Id for a prompt (enclosed in brackets) in the Criteria row of the ItemId column.
8. To verify the query runs correctly, Insert Bakery ItemId B421.
9. Save the query as Query 1 Parameter Query.

Query 2: Group By Query   How many of each bakery item do the chefs need to bake tonight?

1. On the Create tab, in the Query group, click on Query Design.
2. In Design view, select the Inventory and Order tables as the input.
3. Include the following fields in the output: ItemName, Quantity.
4. Use the Totals icon button on the toolbar. Within the Totals category, Group by ItemName. Select Sum category for the Quantity field.
5. Sort Quantity descending.
6. Run and Save the query as Query 2 Chefs Daily Delivery.

Query 3: Calculated Field Query   What is the billing amount of today's delivery orders for each of our customers? Figure 7.2 shows the Query layout.

1. On the Create tab, in the Query group, click on Query Design.
2. In Design view, select the Customer, Inventory, and Order tables as the input.
3. Select the field NameOfEstablishment.
4. Insert a calculated field titled BillingAmount, and multiply [PricePerItem] * [Quantity].
5. Use the Totals icon button on the toolbar, and within the Totals category Group by NameOfEstablishment.
6. Select Sum under Totals category for the BillingAmount field. Sort Billing Amount descending.
7. Run and Save the query as Query 3 Daily Billing Amount.

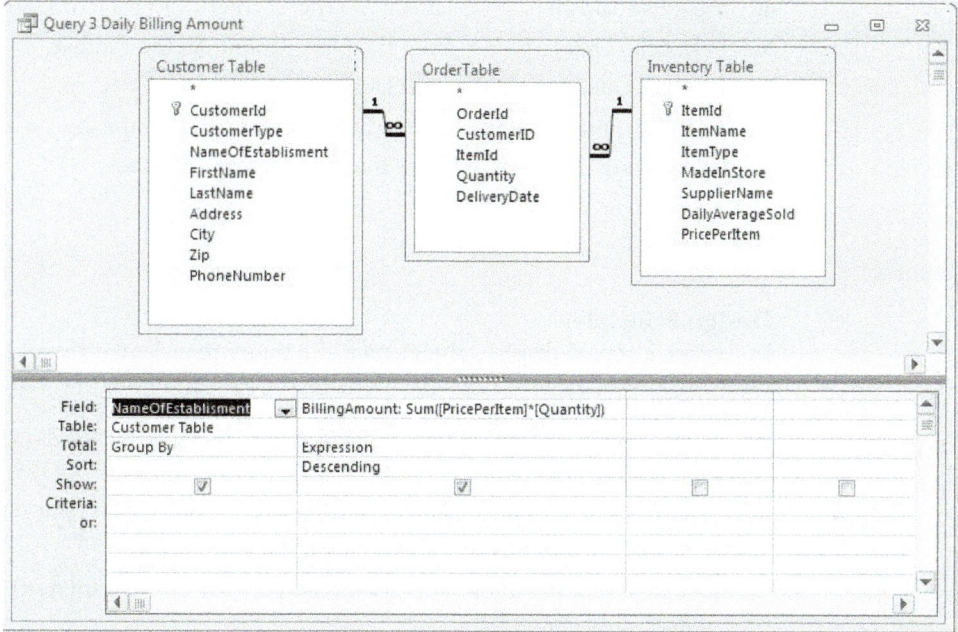

Figure 7.2 Query 3 Layout

Query 4: Make-Table Query To save time and gasoline, the delivery drivers want to split up the deliveries for restaurants only. You need to create a table just for restaurants.

1. On the Create tab, in the Query group, click on Query Design.
2. In Design view, select the Customer table as the input and include all the fields in the output.
3. Enter Restaurant as the criterion in the CustomerType field.
4. Select Make-Table Query from the Query menu on the toolbar.
5. Save the query as Make-Table Restaurant.
6. Run the Make-Table Restaurant query to create the new table.

Query 5: Delete Query One of your suppliers, CupCake Express, called and informed you that they are no longer making strawberry cream cupcakes. You need to delete the orders that have the ItemId B421, which is the strawberry cream cupcake.

1. On the Create tab, in the Query group, click on Query Design.
2. In Design view, select the Order table as the input and include all the fields in the output.
3. Under ItemId within the criteria row, type in ItemId B421.

4. View the datasheet to see if you did this correctly; go back to Design view.
5. Select the Delete Query from the Query menu on the toolbar.
6. Run the Query to activate the Delete Query.
7. Save the query as Delete Query Strawberry Cream Cupcake.
8. Check your Order table to see that it in fact was deleted.

Reports

Design Principle
In Access, a report displays the output of a query in an easy-to-read layout. A report is especially useful to show the output of a total query, grouping the summary information by category.

Implementation
Report 1   Create a report from Query 1 that is based on which customers are requesting a certain bakery item. Figure 7.3 shows parameter report layout.

1. Create a report in Report Wizard based on Query 1 Parameter.
2. Select all available fields.
3. View the data by inventory table.
4. Use landscape orientation.
5. Use the default layout.
6. Title the report "Parameter Report."
7. Create a label (the "Aa" icon) with your name below the title within the header.
8. Insert Bakery ItemId B571.
9. Switch to Layout view and insert value-added features such as text formatting, text alignment, and color shading to increase the readability of the information.
10. Change the date properties to short date within the footer.
11. Save the report as Report 1 Parameter Report.

Report 2   Create a report based on Query 2. This report will show the bakery items chefs need to bake today.

1. Create a report in Report Wizard based on the Query 2 Chefs Daily Delivery.
2. Select all available fields.
3. Use the default layout.
4. Title the report "Chefs Daily Delivery Report".
5. Modify the field text labels appropriately.
6. Create a label (the "Aa" icon) with your name below the title within the header.
7. Switch to Layout view and insert value-added features such as text formatting, text alignment, and color shading to increase the readability of the information.

Parameter Report

Student Name

ItemId	Customer Id	Customer Type	Name Of Establisment	First Name	Phone Number	Delivery Date
B571						
	C130	Restaurant	Organics	Victoria	(619) 837-4632	6/1/2013
	C129	Restaurant	Cranberries	John	(619) 220-3928	6/1/2013
	C125	Restaurant	Spice	Kathrine	(760) 538-5453	6/1/2013

Figure 7.3   Parameter Report

8. Change the date properties to short date within the footer.
9. Save the report as Report 2 Chefs Daily Delivery.

Report 3   Create a report based on Query 3 to show the billing amount of today's delivery orders for each of our customers.

1. Create a report in Report Wizard based on the Query 3 Daily Billing Amount.
2. Select all available fields.
3. Use the default layout.
4. Within the Grouping and Totals menu under the Design menu, insert a totals option to sum the Daily Billing Amount.
5. Title the report "Daily Billing Amount."
6. Create a label (the "Aa" icon) with your name below the title within the header.
7. Switch to Layout view and insert value-added features such as text formatting, text alignment, and color shading to increase the readability of the information.
8. Change the date properties to short date within the footer.
9. Save the report as Report 3 Daily Billing Amount Report.

▶ USING THE DATABASE APPLICATION

1. As the bakery's manager, you want to quickly revise some of the queries.
   a. Using the Parameter Query, which customers ordered the wheat grass?

    b. Modify the Query 3 Daily Billing Amount to show the billing amount for the restaurant customers only. Save query as Restaurant Daily Billing Amount.

    c. Describe how you would revise Query 2 to show the daily delivery for a particular customer.

2. Often, new information requirements arise for the bakery.

    a. Create a query and report for the drivers to deliver the baked goods. Include the necessary information for the drivers to deliver the correct inventory to the correct address. Save the query and the report as Delivery Location.

    b. Describe the steps you need to go through to add a new customer to the database and a new order with several inventory items for that new customer.

    c. Why is referential integrity important in the design of the Up the Hill Bakery database application?

Sun and Beach Clothing
Inventory and Supplier Analysis

ACCESS WORKING CASE: ADVANCED LEVEL

Submission Instructions Complete Case 8 in Access. Answer the questions at the end of this case and ask your instructor for submission instructions.

Preview You are the sales manager of Sun and Beach Clothing Store. This store offers a wide variety of popular beach clothing and accessories. The store is going through a transition period and needs to discontinue a few of the suppliers who have the lowest sales in the store. As the sales manager of the store you need to create various weekly reports on inventory to identify the most popular and least popular items that are sold in the store.

Skill Set

One-to-Many table relationship
Parameter query
Grouping query
Make-Table query
Delete-Table query

Background Sun and Beach Clothing Store, located in Newport, California, carries a wide variety of popular beach clothing and accessories. It carries one of the largest selections of brand-name clothing in the area. The store has a modest database application used to keep track of inventory and supplier information. As the sales manager you need to create various weekly inventory reports. You will review these reports to identify the relative popularity of items so you can decide which suppliers to cancel. You also want to monitor the sales and profits for each brand of clothing and accessories. In addition, you want to make a few changes to the supplier database table: You want to create a separate database table for the supplier of the most popular (best-selling) clothing items, which involves also deleting certain information from the existing supplier table.

▶ CASE ANALYSIS

Output Requirements

The store needs a total of five queries and three reports. You are to create three queries to calculate summary information about sales and profits. You also need three reports to show these query results in a value-added layout. You are to create a query to make a new table and a query to delete fields from the existing inventory table.

Input Requirements

An inventory table and a supplier table for the Sun and Beach Clothing Store database have been created for you. Table 8.1 shows the final information that you need to input in the Inventory table. The Inventory table can be found in the file named Case 8.

▶ DESIGN AND IMPLEMENTATION

Database Table Relationships

Design Principle

Table 8.1 shows the information for three new inventory items. You need to input the three new inventory items into the inventory table. Note that each item has a unique identification code; similarly, each supplier in the Supplier table has a unique identification code. Each supplier provides several different items to the Sun and Beach Clothing Store, which is a one-to-many relationship. To link the Inventory table with the Supplier table, the unique identification code of the supplier is included in each inventory item record. Figure 8.1 shows the one-to-many relationship between the inventory table and the supplier table.

Implementation

1. Open the Access file titled Case 8.

2. Open the Inventory table and the Supplier table and note their structure and content, then close both tables.

3. Open the Inventory table and enter the information shown in Table 8.1.

4. Use the Relationships tool to create a one-to many relationship with referential integrity between the Supplier table and the Inventory table.

Table 8.1 Inventory table

Inventory Id	Inventory Type	Supplier Id	Annual Quantity	Product Price
I0002	Shirts	S0001	230	$29.00
I0023	Accessories	S0003	650	$26.00
I0034	Jackets	S0007	300	$250.00

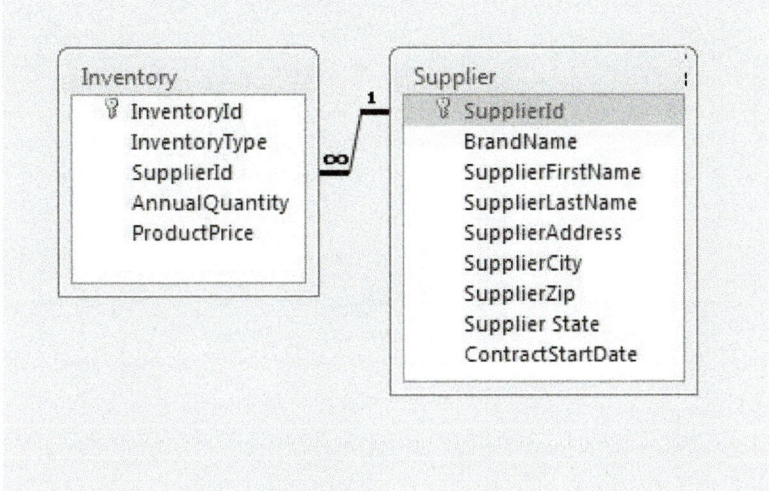

Figure 8.1 One-to-Many Relationship

Queries

Design Principle

A query allows you to select information from several related tables based on search criteria and then perform summary statistics and database processing tasks with the retrieved information.

Implementation

Query 1: Parameter Query You want to create a query to access specific profit information for a particular brand of clothing. The parameter query works best for this type of query, especially if you are just focusing on one product.

1. On the Create tab, in the Query group, click on Query Design.
2. In Design view, select the Inventory and Supplier tables as the input.
3. Include the following fields in the output: BrandName, InventoryType, AnnualQuantity.
4. Include a calculated field for TotalAnnualProfit: [AnnualQuantity] * [ProductPrice].
5. Enter text Brand Name for a prompt (enclosed in brackets) in the Criteria row of the BrandName column.
6. Verify the query runs correctly.
7. Save the query as Query 1 Parameter Query.

Query 2: Calculated Field and Grouping Query You want to run a query to identify which brands are doing well in your store and which brands you might want to consider eliminating. Run a query for the total annual profit for each brand of clothing. Figure 8.2 shows the Design view of Query 2.

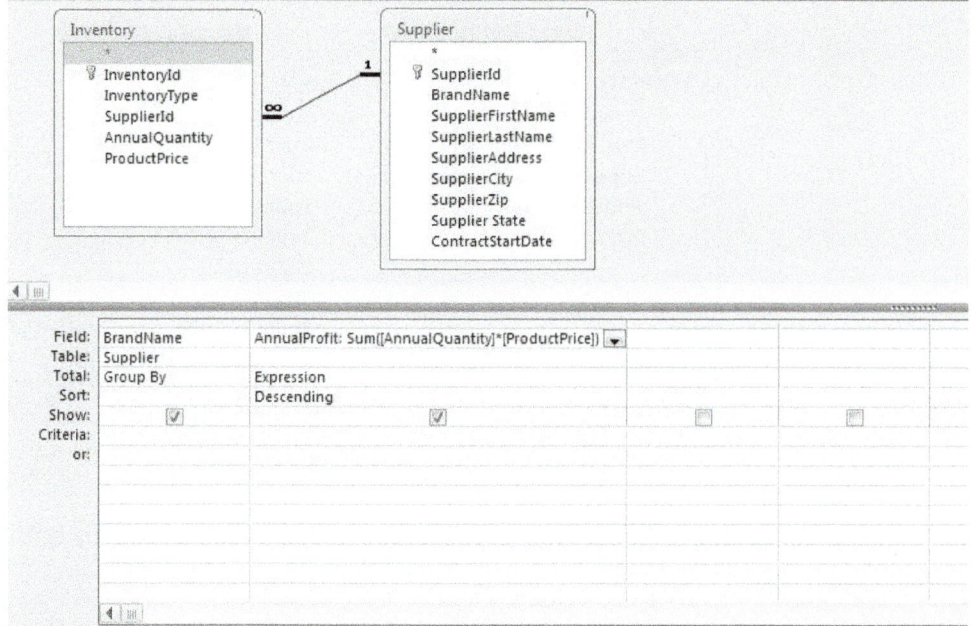

Figure 8.2 Query 2 in Design view

1. On the Create tab, in the Query group, click on Query Design.
2. In Design view, select the Inventory and Supplier tables as the input.
3. Include in the output the BrandName and a calculated field for

    TotalAnnualProfit: [AnnualQuantity] * [ProductPrice].

4. Use the Totals icon button on the toolbar. Within the Totals category select Group by BrandName. Select Sum for the Profit field.
5. Sort by Profit in descending order.
6. Save the query as Query 2 Annual Profit by Brand Name.

Query 3: Calculated Field and Grouping Query   You want to research the annual total quantity sold for each brand.

1. On the Create tab, in the Query group, click on Query Design.
2. In Design view, select the Inventory and Supplier tables as the input.
3. Include the fields BrandName and Annual Quantity in the output.
4. Use the Totals icon button on the toolbar. Within the Totals category select Group by BrandName and select Sum for the AnnualQuantity field.
5. Sort AnnualQuantity in descending order.
6. Insert a Standard number format for AnnualQuantity.
7. Save the query as Query 3 Annual Quantity by Brand Name.

Query 4: Make-Table Query Queries 2 and 3 identified the brand name that is the most profitable. Create a separate table for this brand.

1. On the Create tab, in the Query group, click on Query Design.
2. In Design view, select the Supplier table as the input.
3. Include all the fields in the output.
4. Enter O'Mally as the criterion in the BrandName field.
5. Select Make-Table Query from the Query menu on the toolbar.
6. Save the table as Top Supplier.
7. Save the query as Make-Table Top Supplier, and keep the default settings.
8. Run the query.

Query 5: Delete Query You have received news the supplier for the Burley brand will no longer be a supplier for your business. You need to delete the inventory items from the Burley brand name.

1. On the Create tab, in the Query group, click on Query Design.
2. Use the Inventory table to create a query that includes all fields.
3. Under Supplier Id within the Criteria row, type in Burley (S0003).
4. View datasheet to see if you did this correctly. Go back to Design view.
5. Select the Delete Query from the Query menu on the toolbar.
6. Save the query as Delete-Query Burley.
7. Activate the query by double clicking on the query.
8. Check your inventory table to make sure that it in fact was deleted.

Reports

Design Principle
The information retrieved by a query can be shown in a report layout that increases the readability and usability of the information. A popular use of reports is to summarize information by categories, which is referred to as a *summary report*.

Implementation
Report 1 Create a report based on the Foxy Brand.

1. Create a report in Report Wizard based on Query 1 Parameter.
2. Select all available fields.
3. Use the default layout.
4. Use the landscape page orientation.
5. Choose Foxy at the prompt for Brand Name.
6. Title the report "Parameter Report."
7. Create a label (the "Aa" icon) with your name below the title within the header.

8. Switch to Layout view and insert value added-features such as text formatting, text alignment, and color shading to increase the readability of the information.
9. Change the date properties to short date within the footer.
10. Save the report as Report 1 Parameter Report.

Report 2   Create a report to show the total annual profit for each brand of clothing.

1. Create a report in Report Wizard based on the Query 2 Annual Profit by Brand Name.
2. Select all available fields.
3. Sort by Profit in descending order.
4. Use the default layout.
5. Use the landscape page orientation.
6. Title the report "Annual Profit by Brand Name."
7. Create a label (the "Aa" icon) with your name below the title within the header.
8. Switch to Layout view and insert value-added features such as text formatting, text alignment, and color shading to increase the readability of the information.
9. Change the date properties to short date within the footer.
10. Save the report as Report 2 Annual Profit by Brand Name.

Report 3   Create a report that lists the annual total quantity sold for each brand.

1. Create a report in Report Wizard based on Query 3 Annual Quantity by Brand Name.
2. Select all available fields.
3. Use the default layout.
4. Title the report "Annual Quantity by Brand Name."
5. Create a label (the "Aa" icon) with your name below the title within the header.
6. Switch to Layout view and insert value-added features such as text formatting, text alignment, and color shading to increase the readability of the information.
7. Change the date properties to short date within the footer.
8. Save the report as Report 3 Annual Quantity by Brand Name.

▶ USING THE DATABASE APPLICATION

1. As the clothing store's sales manager, you are interested in enhancing the interactive query capability of the database.
    a. Using Query 1 Parameter Query, what is the total annual profit of the O'Mally brand name? How many different inventory items are there of the O'Mally brand?
    b. Describe how to modify the design of Query 1 to show in the answer only the inventory items for a particular brand that have annual quantities less than 100.

    c. Describe how to modify the design of the Query 1 Parameter Report to show the sum of all the inventory item profit values—that is, the overall profit for the brand.

2. As the sales manager, you need to decide whether to continue with various brands.

    a. Using the Annual Profit by Brand Name query or report, what is the total profit for the Foxy brand? How does the Foxy brand's profit compare to the O'Mally brand's profit?

    b. Using the Annual Quantity by Brand Name query or report, how many items of the O'Mally brand move through inventory annually? How does this compare to the Foxy brand?

    c. Based on your review of these two queries and reports, which brand names would you consider discontinuing, if any?

3. As the sales manager, you realize you need additional information in the database.

    a. Describe the modifications that would be required to add the phone number of each supplier in the database.

    b. Describe the modifications that would be required to add a new supplier to the database.

4. Use the Web find out the definition of an Append query. How could you use the Append query in this database?

5. Search the Web find out the definition of an Up-Date query. How could you use the Up-Date query in this database?

Just Breathe Yoga Center

Instructor and Class Schedule Database

ACCESS WORKING CASE: ADVANCED LEVEL

Submission Instructions Complete Case 9 in Access. Answer the questions at the end of this case and ask your instructor for submission instructions.

Preview You are the operations manager for Just Breathe Yoga Center. The yoga center has seven locations and more than 26 instructors around the western region of the United States. The existing database organizes the class schedules, instructor, and location information. From the database you need to run queries on which locations and classes are the most popular, and you need to monitor the revenue for each yoga center.

Skill Set

One-to-many table relationship
Parameter query
Grouping query
Make-Table query
Delete-Table query

Background Just Breathe Yoga Center started its first studio in Denver, Colorado, and has expanded to other Western states. You have access to the yoga center's database of all the studios, which includes class schedules, location, and employee information. As operations manager, you need to create a parameter query to search particular class schedules for the different locations. You also want to create two queries that identify the Revenue by location and Revenue by class description. The final queries will be a Make-Table Query and a Delete Query.

► CASE ANALYSIS

Output Requirements

You are to create a total of five queries and three reports. Two of the queries are to be a Make-Table query to separate the top instructors and a Delete Query to delete fields from the existing class schedule table.

Input Requirements

Open Access file case 9. The database has been created for you. Table 9.1 displays the information for the last three class schedules. Enter the class schedules in the Class Schedule table. Once you have completed the new entries, create the necessary queries and reports within the processing requirements.

► DESIGN AND IMPLEMENTATION

Class Schedule Table and Database Table Relationships

Design Principle
Table 9.1 shows the information for three different yoga classes offered. You need to input these remaining classes in the Class Schedule table of the database. Note that each class has a unique identification code. Similarly, each instructor in the Instructor table has a unique identification code, and each location in the Location table has a unique identification code. Each instructor teaches several classes, several classes are held in each location, and several instructors can teach at a particular location. To define these one-to-many relationships among the Class, Location, and Instructor tables, the unique identification code of the particular table needs to be included in subsequent table(s).

Implementation
1. Open the Access file titled Case 9.
2. Open the Class Schedule table and enter the information shown in Table 9.1.
3. Use the Relationship tool to create a one-to-many relationship as shown in Figure 9.1, with referential integrity between:
   - LocationId (Location table) and LocationId (Instructor table)
   - LocationId (Location table) and LocationId (Class Schedule table)
   - InstructorId (Instructor table) and InstructorId (Class Schedule table)

Table 9.1 Class Schedule

Class Id	Class Description	Instructor Id	Location Id	Class Time	Class Price	Number of Students
C027	Beginning	T25	L7	1:00 PM	$12.00	20
C028	Advanced	T25	L7	5:00 PM	$13.00	16
C029	Intermediate	T26	L7	8:00 PM	$14.00	14

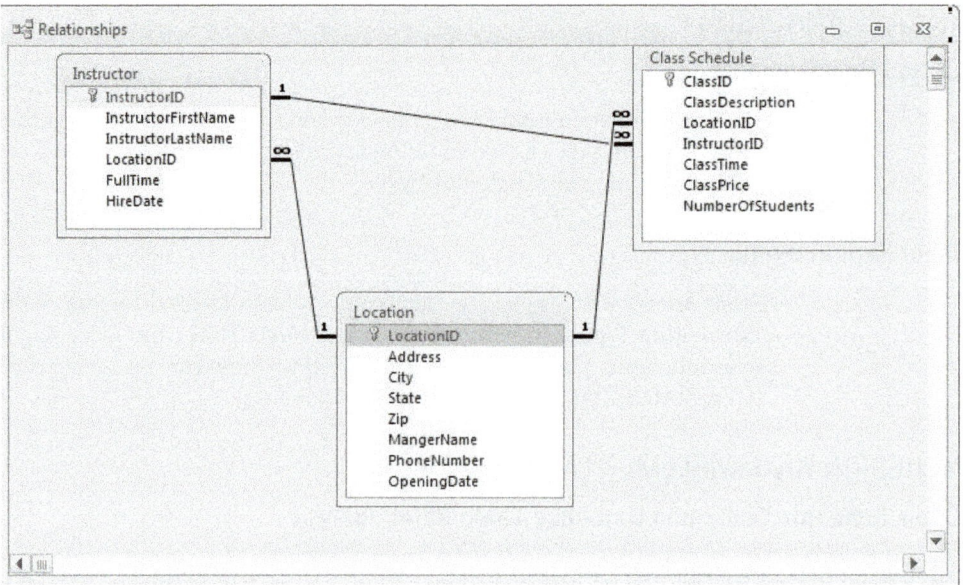

Figure 9.1 One-to-Many Relationships

Queries

Design Principle

A query allows you to select information from several related tables based on search criteria and then perform summary statistics and database processing tasks with the retrieved information.

Implementation

Query 1: Parameter Query   You need to create a Parameter query to have quick access to class information. What are the Class Time, Class Description, and Instructor teaching in a particular city?

1. Create a Query in Design view and include all three tables.
2. In your query include the following fields: ClassDescription, ClassTime, Instructor-FirstName, and City.
3. Enter City Name as the text prompt enclosed in brackets in the Criteria row. This allows the user to view one city at a time.
4. Run the query and type in Denver at the City Name prompt.
5. Save the query as Query 1 Parameter Query.

Query 2: Calculated Field and Grouping Query   You are thinking of adding more classes to the schedule, so you want to research which classes yield the most revenue. What is the total revenue by class description? Figure 9.2 shows Query 2 in Design view.

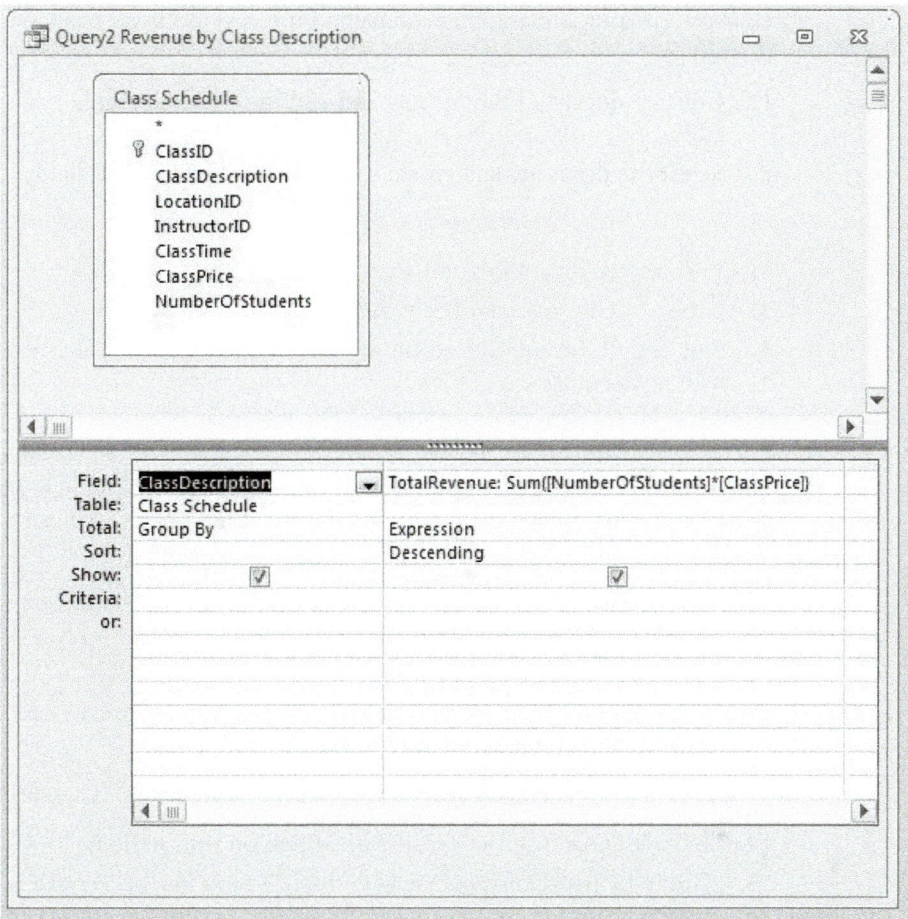

Figure 9.2 Query 2 in Design view

1. Create a query in Design view and add the Class Schedule table.
2. Select the field ClassDescription, and create a total revenue calculated field

    TotalRevenue: NumberOfStudents ∗ ClassPrice.

3. In your query select the Totals icon button on your toolbar.
4. Group by ClassDescription and select Sum for the Revenue field.
5. Sort Revenue in descending order, and format the calculated field as currency with no decimals.
6. Save the query as Query 2 Revenue by Class Description.

Query 3: Calculated Field and Grouping Query　You want to run a query to find out the revenue by location. You want to find out which locations are doing the worst. You might consider creating a marketing campaign for those locations or closing those studios in the future.

1. Create a query in Design view and add the Class Schedule table and the Location table.
2. Select the field City and create a Total revenue calculated field.

   TotalRevenue: [NumberOfStudents] * [ClassPrice].

3. In your query use the Totals icon button on your toolbar.
4. Group by City and select Sum for the TotalRevenue field.
5. Sort TotalRevenue by descending order, and format the calculated field as currency with no decimals.
6. Save the query as Query 3 Revenue by Location.

Query 4: Make-Table Query   Create a new table for the top instructors. You want to give your top instructors seniority and offer them right of first refusal to teach any classes that become available.

1. Create a query in Design view that shows which instructors are the top instructors within all the studios.
2. Include the Instructor table and the Class Schedule table in your query.
3. Insert the following fields: InstructorFirstName, InstructorLastName, ClassTime, and a calculated field for total revenue.

   TotalRevenue: [NumberOfStudents] * [ClassPrice].

4. In your query, use the Totals icon button on your toolbar.
5. Group by InstructorLastName and select Sum for the TotalRevenue field.
6. Sort TotalRevenue by descending order, and format the calculated field as currency with no decimals.
7. Under the Revenue criteria, place a criterion for greater than $300.00, and sort by descending order.
8. Select the Query menu and choose Make-Table Query.
9. Save the new table as Top Instructors.
10. Save the query as Query 4 Make-Table Query.
11. Select Tables from the main menu to check to see if the new table was created.

Query 5: Create a Delete Query   You want to create a query to identify the classes that produce the least revenue and notify the studios that these classes will be cancelled.

1. Create a Query in Design view and select the ClassSchedule table. Insert all fields and create a total revenue calculated field

   TotalRevenue: [NumberOfStudents] * [ClassPrice].

2. For the TotalRevenue field type enter the criterion less than $150.00.

3. Sort by descending order.

4. Select the Query menu and select Delete Query.

5. Save the query as Query 5 Delete Query.

6. Delete the lowest-revenue class times from Class Schedule table by selecting the query you have just saved.

7. Check the Class Schedule table to see if those fields have been deleted.

Reports

Design Principle

Once you have completed and saved each query, you need to create a report for the Parameter Query and the two Group Total Queries.

Implementation

Report 1 Create a report to show the class time, class description, and instructors teaching in Denver.

1. Create a report in Report Wizard based on Query 1 Parameter.

2. Select all available fields.

3. Use the default layout.

4. Use the landscape page orientation.

5. Title the report "Class Description by City."

6. Type in Denver when given the City Name prompt.

7. Create a label (the "Aa" icon) with your name below the title within the header.

8. Switch to Layout view and insert value-added features such as text formatting, text alignment, and color shading to increase the readability of the information.

9. Change the date properties to short date within the footer.

10. Save and rename the report Report 1 Parameter.

Report 2 Figure 9.3 is the layout of Revenue by Class Description Report.

1. Create a report in Report Wizard based on Query 2 Revenue by Class Description.

2. Select all available fields.

3. Use the default layout.

4. Title the report "Revenue by Class Description."

5. Create a label (the "Aa" icon) with your name below the title within the header.

6. Switch to Layout view and insert value-added features such as text formatting, text alignment, and color shading to increase the readability of the information.

7. Change the date properties to short date within the footer.

8. Save the report as Report 2 Revenue by Class Description.

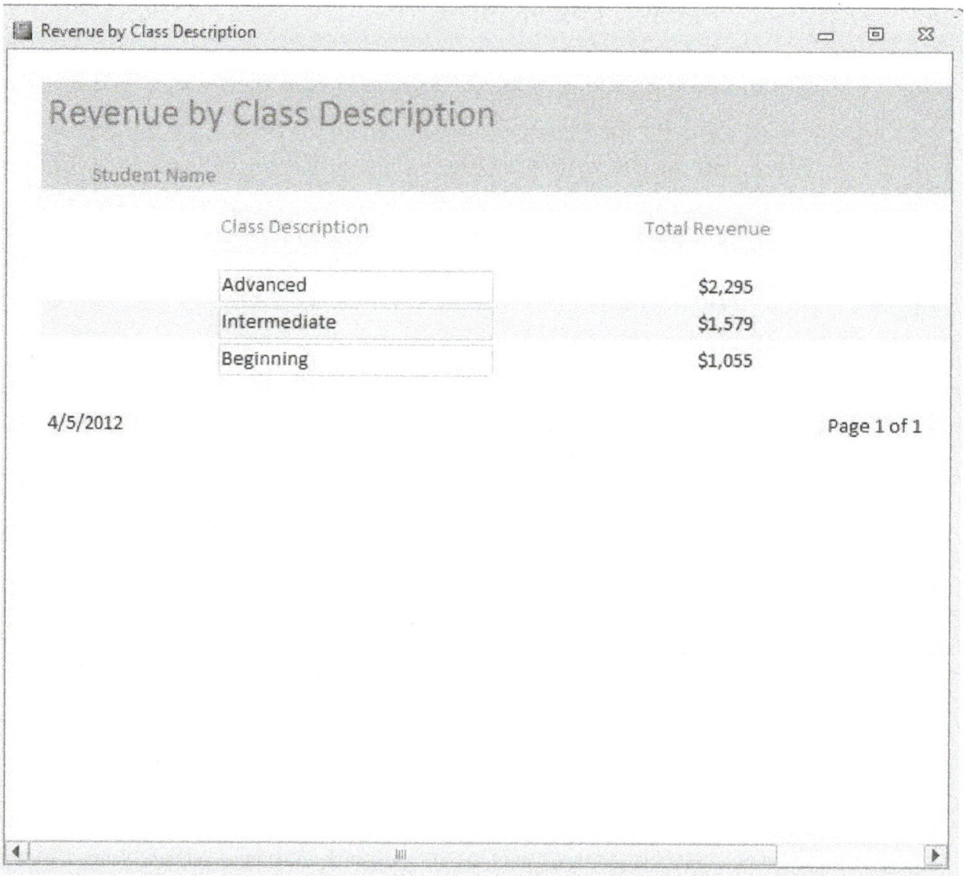

Figure 9.3 Report 2 Layout view

Report 3 Create a report that lists the classes that yield the most revenue.

1. Create a report in Report Wizard based on Query 3 Revenue by Location.
2. Select all available fields.
3. Use the default layout.
4. Title the report "Revenue by Location."
5. Create a label (the "Aa" icon) with your name below the title within the header.
6. Switch to Layout view and insert value-added features such as text formatting, text alignment, and color shading to increase the readability of the information.
7. Change the date properties to short date within the footer.
8. Save the report as Report 3 Revenue by Location.

► USING THE DATABASE APPLICATION

1. As operations manager for the Just Breathe Yoga Center, you are interested in enhancing the interactive query capability of the database.

   a. Refer to Query 1 Parameter. Who are the instructors who teach advanced classes in Denver? In La Jolla?

   b. Describe how to modify the design of the Parameter query and the Parameter report to show also the number of students in each of the classes taught at a particular location.

2. As the operations manager, you need to decide where to offer more classes.

   a. Refer to the Revenue by Class Description query or report. What is the total revenue for each of the three types of yoga classes?

   b. Using the Revenue by Location query or report, visually compare the locations' revenues. Which location has the highest revenue? The lowest revenue?

   c. Based on your review of these two queries or reports, can you decide where more classes should be offered?

   d. Modify Report 2 Revenue by Class Description and Report 3 Revenue by Location to calculate the overall total revenue. (Hint: Use the Sum function from the Totals button in Design view.) Does this modification to the two reports help you decide where more classes should be offered?

   e. Modify Query 2 Revenue by Class Description to show the total number of students in each of the three types of yoga classes. Does adding this information help you decide where more classes should be offered?

3. As the operations manager, you realize you need additional information in the database.

   a. Describe the modifications that would be required to add a new instructor into the database.

   b. Describe how to design a query and report to show the total number of students and the total revenue generated for each full-time instructor. How would the query and report be useful in deciding where to try increasing the number of students?

4. Search the Web to find out the definition of an Append query. How could you use the Append query in this database?

5. Use the Web to find out the definition of an Up-Date query. How could you use the Up-Date query in this database?

Trophy Max

Small-Business Database

ACCESS CAPSTONE

Submission Instructions   Complete the Access Capstone. You will need to start with a blank database for this assignment. Ask your instructor for submission instructions.

Preview   You are a business owner of a trophy and recognition gift store. You offer trophies and awards for corporate, school, and sporting events. Trophy Max provides a wide variety of award types such as plaques, medals, and trophies. You also offer engraving and shipping.

Skill Set

Tables	Queries	Forms	Reports
Table formatting Setting relationships	Calculated field	Form formatting	Report formatting

Background   You have just purchased a small trophy and awards store in Oceanside, California. The business is well established and has been around for many years. The previous owners used an Excel spreadsheet for their store's database. As the new owner you want to transfer their data from Excel into an Access database. The database will have four tables: Existing Customer table, Product table, Supplier table, and Order table. You also want to create forms for each of the tables for your sales team to enter new data when necessary. As store owner of Trophy Max you need to create several weekly reports showing a variety of weekly sales statistics.

▷ CASE ANALYSIS

Output Requirements

You need to create a database application for your business. The prior owners had kept records using Excel. You need to import the Excel spreadsheet information and create four tables: Existing Customer table, Product table, Supplier table, and Order table. You also need to create four input forms based on these tables for easy data entry and editing.

In addition to creating tables and forms you need to run weekly queries and create reports based on the weekly sales information. These queries and reports will help your business become organized and provide efficient customer service.

Input Requirements

The information for the data tables can be found in the Excel spreadsheet titled Access_Capstone. All four data tables need to be imported into Access from the Excel spreadsheet. As you import your data you want to approve the data to be indexed as "yes, no duplicates."

► DESIGN AND IMPLEMENTATION

Tables

Design Principle
The layout of the four tables consists of the first row composed of field names, followed by rows that represent a record of information for each particular table.

Implementation
You need to consider the formatting of these tables and using the field properties in Design view appropriately. Make sure you specify proper field sizes for each field, as well as designing lookup wizards where needed. Insert Input Masks for easy entry of phone numbers, and correctly define the data type for each field.

Database Table One-to-Many Relationships

Design Principle
Note that each of the four tables includes a field that has a unique identification code: Customer Id, Supplier Id, Product Id, and Order Id. You need to create the correct relationships between the tables. Figure AC.1 shows the one-to-many relationships among the tables.

Implementation

1. Open the Customer, Order, Supplier, and Product tables. Note their structure and content, then close all tables.
2. Use the Relationships tool to create the one-to-many relationships among the tables, as shown in Figure AC.1. Include all four tables within the workspace of the relationship tool.
3. Create a one-to-many relationship with referential integrity between the Supplier table and the Product table.
4. Create a one-to-many relationship with referential integrity between the Customer table and the Order table.
5. Create a one-to-many relationship with referential integrity between the Product table and the Order table.

Figure AC.1 One-to-Many Relationship

Forms

Design Principle

Database application users can use predesigned data entry forms to improve data accuracy when entering and modifying database tables.

Implementation

The form layout needs to include visual features such as titles and control buttons for adding and deleting information and for closing the form in an easy and error-free way. You also need to label your buttons correctly within the property sheet.

Order Form The layout for the data entry order form is shown in Figure AC.2.

1. Create the order table within the Form Wizard.
2. Include all fields of the Order table, and include Product Cost from the Product table. You need to add three calculated fields within the order form: Product Amount, Delivery Cost, and Total Amount Owed.
3. The Product Amount formula can be computed by multiplying [Product Cost] * [Quantity].
4. The Delivery Cost formula can be computed by multiplying [Product Amount] by 10% (create the proper label for Product Amount).
5. The Total Amount Owed formula can be computed by [Delivery Cost] * [Product Amount] (create the proper label for Delivery Cost).

Figure AC.2 Order Form Layout

Queries

Design Principle

A query allows you to retrieve, or select, information from any combination of fields in one or more tables based on a criterion. Figure AC.3 shows an example of a query in Design view.

Implementation

Query 1   You want to mail your new clients a list of all the awards that cost less than or equal to $30.00.

1. In Query Design view, select the Product table as the input.
2. Include the following fields: Product Name, Product Type, Product Cost.
3. Create a criterion for the Product Cost field: less than or equal to 30.
4. Sort Product Cost in ascending order.
5. Save the query as Query 1 Products for $30.00 or Less.

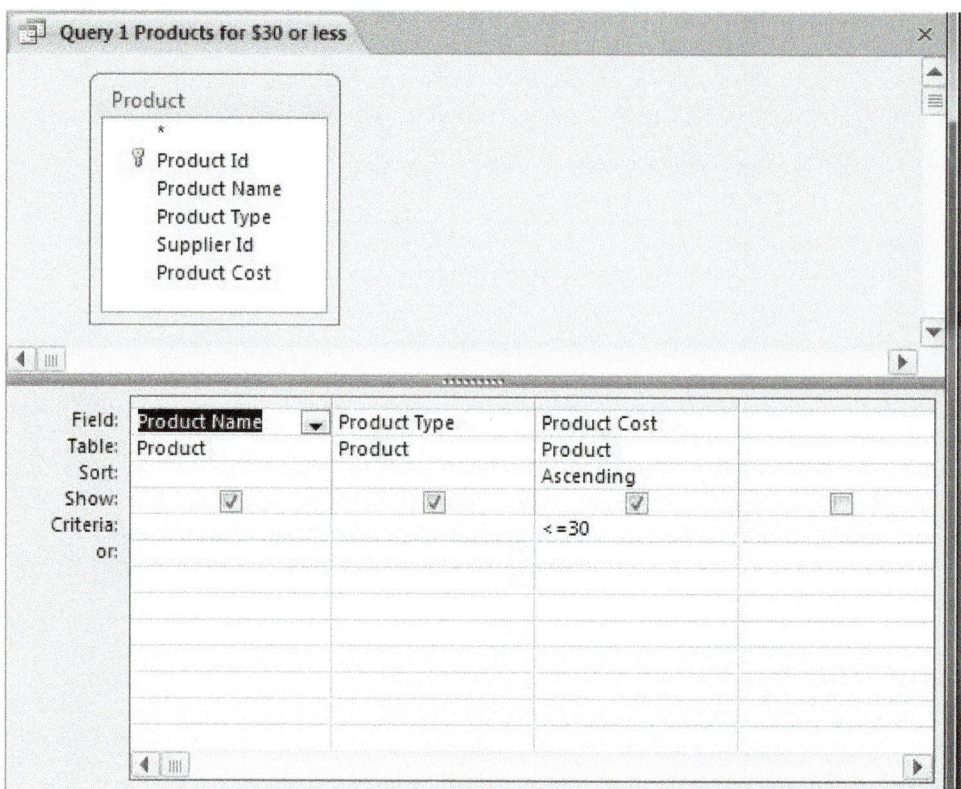

Figure AC.3   Example Query in Design view

Query 2   You want to create a delivery date query so that you can get your awards out on time. Create a query that lists your customer delivery information and then sort it by delivery date.

1. In Query Design view, select the Order table and Customer table as the input.
2. Include the following fields from the Customer table: First Name, Last Name, Address, City, State, Zip Code.
3. Include the Delivery Date field from the Order table.
4. Sort Delivery Date in ascending order.
5. Save the query as Query 2 Delivery Date for July.

Query 3   You want to know which clients requested more than 30 awards in a single order, and you want to show the delivery date.

1. In Design view, select the Order table and the Customer table as the input.
2. Include the following fields from the customer table: First Name, Last Name, Phone Number.
3. Include the following fields from the order table: Purpose of Event, Quantity, Delivery Date.
4. Create a criterion for the Quantity field for greater than or equal to 30.
5. Sort Delivery Date by ascending order.
6. Save the query as Query 3 Orders Over 30 Units per Client.

Reports

Design Principle
In Access, a report displays the retrieved information of a query in an attractive, easy-to-read format. In addition to the retrieved information, a report can have several value-added features including a title, date, and footer. You can create one or more reports from a saved query.

Implementation
Report 1   You would like to create a report based on Query 1. The report will show a list of all the awards that cost less than $30.00.

1. Create a report in Report Wizard based on Query 1.
2. Report Wizard asks if you want to sort. Sort Product Cost in ascending order.
3. Title the report "Products for $30 or Less," change the font color of the title, and center the title. Create a label with your name below the title within the header.
4. Switch to Layout view and insert value-added features such as text formatting, text alignment, and color shading to increase the readability of the information.

5. Change the date properties to short date within the footer.
6. Save the report as Report 1 Products for $30 or Less.

Report 2 You would like to create a report based on Query 2. The report will show a list of delivery dates for the awards to be delivered in July. Figure AC.4 shows the layout for Report 2.

1. Create a report in Report Wizard based on Query 2.
2. Report Wizard asks how you want to view your data. View by order.
3. Report Wizard asks if you want to sort. Sort by Delivery Date in ascending order.
4. Page orientation should be landscape.
5. Title the report "Delivery Dates for July" and center the title.
6. Create a label with your name below the title within the header.
7. Switch to Layout view and insert value-added features such as text formatting, text alignment, and color shading to increase the readability of the information.
8. Change the date properties to short date within the footer.
9. Save the report as Report 2 Delivery Dates for July.

🖼 Delivery Date

Delivery Dates for July

Student Name

Delivery Date	First Name	Last Name	Address	City	Stat	Zip
7/1/2013	Brian	Aune	1420 Grand Ave	San Diego	CA	92106
7/2/2013	Patrick	Ruscigno	4944 Cass St UNIT 30	Oceanside	CA	92054
7/2/2013	Chris	Armstrong	1612 Chalcedony St	Oceanside	CA	92054
7/8/2013	Melanie	Hill	3993 Jewell St	San Diego	CA	92101
7/8/2013	Fernanda	Weindel	1235 Parker Pl UNIT :	Oceanside	CA	92054
7/9/2013	Patrick	Ruscigno	4944 Cass St UNIT 30	Oceanside	CA	92054
7/9/2013	David	D'Elia	3930 Ingraham St AP	San Diego	CA	92104
7/10/2013	Daniel	Nieto	4005 Riviera Dr	Oceanside	CA	92054
7/13/2013	Martin	Peterson	1540 Oliver Ave # A	San Marcos	CA	92069
7/17/2013	Crystal	Ursillo	5156 Dawes St	Oceanside	CA	92054
7/18/2013	Gary	Ealy	1761 Hornblend St	Oceanside	CA	92054
7/18/2013	David	Wickline	929 Law St	Carlsbad	CA	92008
7/19/2013	Marc	Stone	1519 Felspar St	Oceanside	CA	92054
7/19/2013	Daniel	Nieto	4005 Riviera Dr	Oceanside	CA	92054
7/20/2013	Tim	Green	4667 Ocean Blvd	Oceanside	CA	92054
7/20/2013	Scott	Battles	721 Wilbur Ave	Oceanside	CA	92054
7/20/2013	Crystal	Ursillo	5156 Dawes St	Oceanside	CA	92054
7/20/2013	Tim	Green	4667 Ocean Blvd	Oceanside	CA	92054

Figure AC.4 Layout for Report 2

Report 3   You would like to create a report based on Query 3. The report will list orders that include 30 or more awards for a single client. You also want to keep track of the delivery date.

1.   Create a report in Report Wizard based on Query 3.
2.   Report Wizard asks how you want to view your data. View by Order.
3.   Report Wizard asks if you want to sort. Sort by Quantity in ascending order.
4.   Page orientation should be landscape.
5.   Title the report "Orders Over 30 Units per Client" and center the title. Create a label with your name below the title within the header.
6.   Switch to Layout view and insert value-added features such as text formatting, text alignment, and color shading to increase the readability of the information.
7.   Change the date properties to short date within the footer.
8.   Save the report as Report 3 Orders Over 30 Units per Client.

► USING THE DATABASE APPLICATION

1.   Realizing the convenience of using a combination of a query to ask a question and a form to show the retrieved information in a value-added layout, you now have several ideas for additional queries and forms.

   a.   Create a query and report that show Oceanside delivery dates after July 10th. Save the query and report as Oceanside Delivery after July 10th. Make sure to include relevant fields from the database in the output, but also make sure you do not include fields that are not meaningful for the query. How does this report help you schedule deliveries?

   b.   Create a query and report that show which corporate clients have their credit cards on file. Save the query and report as Clients Credit Card on File. How can this report help you in billing your customers?

   c.   Create a query and report to show how many trophies we need to make for baseball. Insert a Sum function in the report to show the grand total. Save the query and report as Baseball Trophies. How does this type of report help you plan your orders to suppliers?

2.   You are interested in enhancing the interactive query capability of the database.

   a.   Create a parameter query and report to show the order information of customers who have placed an order for a particular type of product. (Hint: The criterion is the Product Type field.) Include relevant fields from the database, but make sure you do not include fields that are not meaningful for the query. Title the query and the report; Customer order by Product type.

   b.   Create a parameter query and report to show the information regarding the products on order for any particular supplier. (Hint: The criterion is CompanyName.) Title the query and the report; Products on Order by supplier.

3. You want to use the database to evaluate the overall status of this month's business.

   a. What is the total value of orders this month for customers located in San Diego? Describe how you used the database to answer the question.

   b. Which customers have ordered crystal products this month? Describe how you used the database to answer the question.

   c. What products have been ordered this month by customers located in the 92054 zip code? Describe how you used the database to answer the question.

   d. Describe the necessary steps to add a new supplier with two new products to the database.

PART II

DEVELOPING A SPREADSHEET APPLICATION

A spreadsheet application is a software tool used to analyze a situation or solve a problem by manipulating numeric information. Think of a spreadsheet application as a numeric representation, or model, of a situation that a person can use to calculate answers. Many business situations can be structured as spreadsheets that provide business professionals with an effective way of supporting their analysis and decision-making needs.

Just as you did with developing a database application, you should follow a three-phase approach to create a spreadsheet application: analysis, design, and implementation.

In the analysis phase, you want to understand as well as you can the intended purpose of the person who will be using the spreadsheet, especially the desired output. Also, you want to identify the required numeric inputs and assumptions of the spreadsheet. Finally, you need to identify the required processing, or calculations, the spreadsheet needs to perform with the inputs to produce the desired output. Each of the following cases presents the input, processing, and output requirements. In the real world you determine these requirements through interviews with the intended users of the spreadsheet application.

In the design phase, you need to decide how to lay out the spreadsheet's input, processing, and output features identified in your analysis. A well-designed spreadsheet application is easy to use and produces correct results. There are many design guidelines you can follow to make sure the input and output features are clear and easy to use and the calculations are correct. These design guidelines are discussed briefly as you go through the spreadsheet cases.

During the implementation phase you use a spreadsheet program, such as Excel, to create, or code, the spreadsheet application electronically. In the following spreadsheet cases, you use Excel to code the appropriate numeric and text input information, the processing formulas, and the output features such as tables and charts and to apply value-added design features to improve the readability and usability of the spreadsheet. Very importantly, you need to edit your spreadsheet by correcting any mistakes, especially in the formulas. Also, you should include appropriate user instructions and documentation in the spreadsheet application. Several coding, editing, and documentation approaches are discussed briefly in the following spreadsheet cases.

After the spreadsheet application is developed, it is employed to support the user's decision making. Often a user wants to change the value of one or more input variables to see the effect on the output variables, also called what-if analysis. Several what-if analysis techniques are discussed briefly in the spreadsheet cases.

CHAPTER 4

Excel—Spreadsheet Basics

Up the Hill Bakery
Payroll Analysis

EXCEL TEACHING CASE: BEGINNING LEVEL

Submission Instructions Complete Case 10 in Excel. Answer the questions at the end of this case and insert the answers on an Answer Sheet within the Case 10 Excel spreadsheet. Ask your instructor for submission instructions.

Preview As the human resources director for the bakery you will be managing the payroll spreadsheet for the employees at the bakery. The data collected on the employees will help you analyze if the bakery can increase efficiency by improving their operational effectiveness within payroll. As part of the Human Resources department you serve an important role in support activity in the Porter's Value Chain Model.

Skill Set

Format spreadsheet
Absolute reference
Sum, maximum, minimum functions
Date function
Goal seek (question at end of case)
If function
Vlookup table
AutoFilter
Center merge
Chart (question at end of case)

Background Jack and his wife Susan own a small French bakery in Chula Vista, California. Their customers are local residents and other small restaurants around the city. Their store delivers fresh bread and pastries to their customers, and they also serve breakfast and lunch in the bakery.

The restaurant is fully staffed 6 hours a day, 7 days a week. The chefs and managers are usually there 8 hours a day, and the drivers are usually there from 6:00 AM to 3:30 PM. Jack and Susan have 13 employees. Each employee earns an hourly wage. Each employee invests in a pretax retirement account based on a percentage of their regular pay.

▶ CASE ANALYSIS

Output Requirements

Create a spreadsheet application for the weekly payroll. You will need to calculate regular pay, retirement contribution, pay after pretax deduction, social security, federal tax, and net pay for all the employees. The owners would like to see all the payroll information arranged on one worksheet.

Input Requirements

As you open the student file for Case 10 you will find information about the 13 employees. The spreadsheet contains two assumption boxes. These boxes will help you calculate the data needed to complete the payroll.

Processing Requirements

Table 10.1 provides you the formulas you need to calculate the payroll information for each employee.

▶ DESIGN AND IMPLEMENTATION

Figure 10.1 shows the desired one-worksheet layout of the spreadsheet application. Note the rectangular layout of the payroll report comprising input and processing sections, with the entire rectangle considered as the payroll report, or output. Also note the design of the assumptions, or parameters, area. The assumptions are organized into two rectangles, one for each of the types of assumptions needed for the application.

Documentation

Design Principle

In Figure 10.1, the column headings and other text labels clarify the meaning of the numbers shown in the payroll report and the assumptions area. Similarly the value-added features, such as text formatting and alignment, merge and center, and color shading, increase the readability of the information. A title and date for the report would orient the user to the purpose of the spreadsheet application.

Implementation

Use Figure 10.1 as a guide. Focus on using the value-added features mentioned above. Use the Spelling tool to check for inadvertent typographical errors. Experiment with different fonts and color shading, but consistently apply your final choice. Make sure you align titles and column headings appropriately.

Input Area

Design Principle

The employee information input area is arranged as a rectangular area in which each row represents a particular employee and each column represents a characteristic of each employee. Input arranged all together in a rectangular area is referred to as *batch input*. Similarly, the assumptions area is rectangular as well to organize two sets of assumptions needed for the payroll application. Note the assumed values (also referred to as *parameter values*) in the Retirement Scale rectangle are arranged in ascending order, each row representing a range of payroll values and their corresponding tax rate. Value-added features, such as line border and shading, make each input area easy to recognize.

Implementation

Use Table 10.1 and Figure 10.1 to help you understand the parameter values and to enter the employees' input data correctly. Make sure you format the numeric cells, choosing the appropriate Number, Currency, or Percentage format.

Table 10.1 Payroll Formulas

Payroll Component	Formula	Comments
Regular pay	(Hours worked * Hourly wage)	
Retirement contribution	(Vlookup function) * Regular Pay	Vlookup is based on the Retirement Scale assumption box 2 Use absolute reference for the Retirement Contribution scale.
Pay after pretax deductions	Regular Pay − Retirement Contribution	
Social Security	Pay after pretax deductions * Social Security tax	Use absolute reference for the Social Security tax.
Federal tax	If Statement = Logical test: Pay after pretax deduction * 52 > Annual Federal income tax baseline (assumption box 1) True: Pay after pretax deduction * Assumption box 1, Tax bracket 1 False: Pay after pretax deduction * Assumption box 1, Tax bracket 2	52 weeks in the year determines the employee's approximate annual salary.
Net pay	(Pay after deductions) − (Social Security + Federal tax)	
Total, Max, Min, Average		Insert the formulas for Total, Average, Maximum, Minimum, statistics for Hours Worked, Regular Pay, and Net Pay in the worksheet.

					Up the Hill Bakery					
					Payroll Report					
					Date					
Employees	Job Position	Hours Worked	Hourly Wage	Regular Pay	Retirement Contribution	Pay After Pre-Tax Deductions	Social Security Tax	Federal Tax	Net Pay
Jack Grey	Chef	45	$ 15						
Susan Grey	Chef	40	$ 15						
Mary Wright	Chef	35	$ 10						
John Berry	Cashier	33	$ 10						
Collyn Bear	Cashier	32	$ 10						
Chris Hill	Wait Staff	23	$ 7						
Laura Godwin	Wait Staff	30	$ 7						
Samantha Collins	Wait Staff	34	$ 7						
Ed Loyd	Wait Staff	25	$ 7						
Steve Little	Driver	28	$ 8						
Mike Nitsch	Driver	42	$ 8						
Gwen Manchester	Manager	36	$ 15						
Stephanie Baker	Manager	50	$ 15						
Total									
Average									
Maximum									
Minimum									

Assumptions #1 Tax Information	
Social Security Tax	6.2%
Federal Tax Annual Income Baseline	$ 34,500
Income Tax Bracket #1	25%
Income Tax Bracket #2	15%

Assumption Box #2 Retirement Contribution Scale	
Regular Pay	Retirement Percentage
0	2.0%
$ 400.00	3.0%
$ 800.00	4.0%

▶ ▶| **Weekly Payroll** / AnswerSheet / Chef's Data / Laura Godwin / 🔲

Figure 10.1 Payroll Report Layout

Processing Area

Design Principle

The layout of the payroll calculations is arranged as a rectangle, with rows of calculations corresponding to the employee information input rows. Similarly, the statistics calculations are arranged in rectangular fashion corresponding to the appropriate variable columns. The formulas must be correct; otherwise the spreadsheet application will calculate incorrect answers and be of little value to the user. After you create or copy a formula, you should check to make sure the answer is correct. All the numbers should be formatted consistently to improve readability.

Implementation

Use Table 10.1 to help you think about the formulas you need to enter for each employee. There are two ways you could enter the formulas. One way is to enter the Regular Pay formula for the first employee, Jack Grey, verify that the formula is correct, and then copy the formula to the other employees; then repeat the procedure for each of the other six variables. A second way is to enter the formulas for Jack Grey, verify that the formulas are correct, and then copy them all at once to the other employees. Make sure you do not type the parameter values in the formulas but rather use the parameter cell addresses in the formulas. Also, use absolute cell addressing for the parameter cells so you can copy the formulas correctly. Make sure you use the appropriate statistical functions for the formulas in the statistical summary area in the bottom rows of the report. Use the Audit Formulas tool to verify that you have entered all the formulas correctly. Make sure you think about whether or not the formulas are calculating appropriate values.

▶ USING THE SPREADSHEET APPLICATION

As the bakery's human resources manager, you can use the weekly payroll spreadsheet application to analyze the payroll budget and answer a variety of managerial what-if questions. On a new worksheet in the same workbook create another worksheet, named AnswerSheet, for answering the following questions. Where appropriate, create a formula to calculate the correct answer. Before answering each question, reset the Weekly Payroll worksheet to its original values.

1. For the current week, what were the total hours worked by the employees and what was their average net pay?

2. You are considering some changes for some particular employees.

   a. If Jack Grey worked 40 hours per week and got a raise to $25 per hour, what would be his net pay?

   b. Compared to the current week, if next week Samantha Collin's hourly wage was raised to $10 but she worked just 30 hours, what would be the difference in her net pay?

   c. The bakery is considering having employees contribute a higher percentage of their regular pay to their retirement. What would be the new retirement amount for Mike Nitsch, Gwen Manchester, and Stephanie Baker, if the retirement percentage was increased 0.50% for each of the three regular pay categories?

3. You want to remember how certain things are calculated in the payroll report. Insert a comment in the cell of the Federal Tax baseline number in assumption box 1 explaining how the IF statement is used to calculate the employees' federal tax withholding.

4. You want to visualize the payroll report's information, comparing employees in a variety of ways.

   a. Create a stacked bar chart to compare the three chefs, showing each chef's retirement contribution, and net pay values. Move the chart to a new worksheet and name the worksheet an appropriate title. Include value-added features such as a title, x-axis and y-axis titles, legend, and color scheme.

   b. Create an appropriate pie chart in its own worksheet showing Laura Godwin's retirement contribution, Social Security, federal tax, and net pay. Use value-added features such as descriptive chart title and percentage data labels. Move the chart to a new worksheet and name the chart worksheet Laura Godwin.

5. As the human resources manager, you are interested in exploring various what-if situations. Use the Goal Seek tool to calculate the answers to the following questions.

   a. Collyn Bear would like to have a weekly net pay of $500. How many hours does she need to work to earn that amount?

6. As the human resources manager you need to optimize the payroll of your managers by correcting the overlap hours for Manager on Duty. The total amount of time you need for each manager is 30 hours a week. What is the amount that you would save in net pay on a weekly basis and over the course of the year if you implemented this strategy?

7. You are thinking of scheduling one driver in the morning and one driver in late afternoon for a total of 3 hours a day for each driver (7 days a week). What is the amount you would save in regular pay on a weekly basis and over a course of the year if you implemented this strategy?

8. After using the weekly payroll spreadsheet you would like to slightly modify it to improve its usability.

   a. Move the two rectangles comprising the assumptions area from the right side to below the payroll report. Use the Audit tool to verify that the cell references in the formulas have been modified correctly.

   b. Modify the payroll spreadsheet to include a column that shows the total Social Security and federal taxes. Create the appropriate formula and modify the Net Pay formula.

Celebrations for Charity
Break-Even Analysis
EXCEL WORKING CASE: BEGINNING LEVEL

Submission Instructions   Complete Case 11 in Excel. Answer the questions at the end of this case and insert the answers on an Answer Sheet within the Case 11 Excel spreadsheet. Ask your instructor for submission instructions.

Preview   You work in Finance, which takes care of the event budgets for the year. Each event is outsourced to two main companies—a catering company and a security company—and you want to find out if the yearly scheduled events are turning a profit. As part of the finance team your objective is to create a break-even analysis spreadsheet, which will allow you to see the difference between total revenue and total expenses paid for each event. You will be analyzing the spreadsheet to find out your profit margins to increase revenue.

Skill Set

Format spreadsheet
Absolute reference
Sum, maximum, minimum functions
Date function
Goal seek (question at end of case)
If function
Vlookup table
AutoFilter
Center merge
Chart (question at end of case)

Background   Celebrations for Charity is a nonprofit organization in southern California that donates their profits to various causes around the geographic region. Each summer they produce five annual events: Prom Dress Dinner, Battle of the Chefs, Fun in the Sun Fashion Show, Bike Wine Country, and Canine Best-In-Show. They are planning their upcoming event schedule, and the managers hope to raise more money this year than in past years. To do this, they need to decide how many tickets they must sell for each event to break even and to make a profit.

▶ CASE ANALYSIS

Output Requirements

Create a spreadsheet application that Celebrations for Charity can use to calculate the expected sales, expenses, and net profit for the five summer events It has planned on the schedule. It wants to view all the information on one worksheet. Figure 11.1 shows the desired layout of the break-even analysis worksheet.

Input Requirements

Each event has an event price code; this code identifies the price per ticket depending on the type of event. For example, if the event is a gold event the tickets cost $375.00 each. Table 11.1 shows the event status and the corresponding ticket prices. When completing the spreadsheet, use this as the Vlookup table to determine the price per ticket.

Celebrations for Charity assumes initially that the expenses for food and beverages, venue are a certain percentage of total sales for each of the events. Table 11.2 shows these assumptions.

The cost of security and staff is determined by how many tickets are sold per event. A predetermined ticket threshold determines the percentage of cost which then is multiplied by total sales. Table 11.3 shows these assumptions.

Processing Requirements

Table 11.4 shows the formulas you need to use in the spreadsheet application.

Table 11.1   Event Status Price Code (Assumption Box 1)

Event Type	Ticket Price
Diamond	$150
Gold	$375
Platinum	$450

Table 11.2   Cost Assumptions based on Total Sales (Assumption Box 2)

Cost of Food and Beverage	20% of total sales
Cost of Venue	22% of total sales

Table 11.3   Staff and Security Cost Assumptions based on Total Sales (Assumption Box 3)

Ticket Threshold	700	
	Less than threshold	Greater than threshold
Cost of Staff	11% of total sales	18% of total sales
Cost of Security	5% of total sales	10% of total sales

	A	B	C	D	E	F	G
1		Celebration for Charity Break-Even Analysis					
2		Date					
3		Student					
4		Prom Dress Dinner	Battle of the Chefs	Fashion Show	Bike Wine Country	Best-In-Show	
5	Sales						
6	Tickets Sold	700	800	300	225	725	
7	Event Status						
8	Price Per Ticket						
9	Total Sales						
10							
11	Expenses						
12	Food & Beverage						
13	Venue						
14	Staff						
15	Security						
16	Total Expenses						
17	Net Profit						
18							
19	Event Status Price Code Assumption box #1			Cost Assumptions box #2			
20	Diamond	$ 150.00		Cost of Food and Beverage based on Total Sales		20%	
21	Gold	$ 375.00		Cost of Venue based on Total Sales		22%	
22	Platinum	$ 450.00					
23							
24	Staff and Security Assumption box #3						
25	Ticket Threshold	700					
26		less than threshold	greater than threshold				
27	Cost of Staff	11%	18%				
28	Cost of Security	5%	10%				
29							

| ◄ ◄ ► ►| **Break-Even Analysis** / AnswerSheet / TtlSales vs. TtlExpenses Chart / Expenses Chart / Total M

Figure 11.1 Design Layout

▷ DESIGN AND IMPLEMENTATION

Figure 11.1 shows the desired one-worksheet layout of the spreadsheet application. Note the rectangular layout of the input, processing, and output sections and the three rectangles comprising the assumptions area.

Documentation

Review the column headings, one for each of the five events; also review the row labels, one for each of the sales and expenses line items. Insert the value-added design features, such as text formatting and alignment, merge and center, color shading, and cell borders to increase the readability of the information. Make sure you type a

Table 11.4   Break-Even Analysis Formulas

Costs and Revenues	Formula
Price per ticket	Vlookup function is based on the event status price code (assumption box 1)
Total sales	Price per ticket ∗ tickets sold
Food and beverage expense	Total sales ∗ cost of food and beverage (assumption box 2)
Venue expense	Total sales ∗ cost of venue (assumption box 2)

Staff expense	IF function:
	   Logical test: Greater than 700 tickets sold (assumption box 3)
	   True: 18% ∗ total sales
	   False:11% ∗ total sales

Security expense	If function:
	   Logical Test: Greater than 700 tickets sold (assumption box 3)
	   True: 10% ∗ total sales
	   False: 5% ∗ total sales

Total expenses	Sum of expenses
Net profit	Total sales − total expenses

relevant title for the break-even analysis report and use the Date function to show the current date below the title.

Input Area

Enter the value for the number of tickets sold and the Event Status for each of the five events; also, enter the value of the parameters in the three assumption areas. Make sure you format the numeric values appropriately.

Processing Area

Use Table 11.4 to help you with the formulas you need to enter for each line item of the break-even analysis. Make sure you reference the appropriate parameter cells in your formulas and use absolute cell addressing for the parameter cells so you can copy them easily. Think about whether the formula values are reasonable and use the Audit Formulas tool to verify that you have entered them correctly.

▷ USING THE SPREADSHEET APPLICATION

As an analyst on the company's finance team, you need use the break-even analysis spreadsheet to explore a variety of what-if scenarios. On a new worksheet in the same workbook, create another worksheet, named AnswerSheet, for answering the following questions. Where appropriate, create a formula to calculate the correct answer. Before answering each question, reset the Break-Even Analysis worksheet to its original values.

1. As an analyst, you want to know the value of some important financial indicators.
    a. What was the total number of tickets sold and what was the total net profit for all five events?

    b. What was the average cost for food and beverages for all five events?

    c. Which event was the most profitable? The least profitable?

2. The financial team is discussing how changing some of the assumptions would affect the current events' profitability.

    a. What would be the total sales for the Fashion Show event if the Gold ticket pricing increased to $400?

    b. What would be the total net profit of the three Diamond events (Prom Dress Dinner and Battle of the Chefs) if the ticket price had been $250?

    c. The importance of good security is an increasing concern at events. The financial team proposes increasing the cost of security to 8% and 12% depending on how many tickets are sold below or above 700. What would be the increase in total expenses and decrease in total net profit?

    d. Which would result in a higher total net profit for the five events: changing the cost of food and beverage to 18% or changing the cost of venue to 20%?

3. You need to visualize the break-even analysis in a presentation to the financial team.

    a. Compare the five events, showing the total sales and total expenses for each. Use a column chart including appropriate value-added features. Move the chart to a separate sheet and name the sheet Ttl Sales vs. Ttl Expenses Chart.

    b. Compare the four expense categories of the five events. Use a column chart including appropriate value-added features. Move the chart to a separate sheet and name the sheet Expense Chart.

    c. Show the percentage of total net profit accounted for by each of the five events. Use a pie chart with appropriate value-added features. Move the chart to a separate sheet and name the sheet Net Profit Chart.

4. The financial team wants to explore several what-if scenarios. Use the Goal Seek tool to calculate the answers to the following questions.

    a. For the Prom Dress Dinner, how many tickets need to be sold for a net profit of $15,000?

    b. What percentage of Cost of Food and Beverage is needed to increase the Battle of the Chefs event's net profit by 10%? (Hint: Create a formula to calculate the 10% increase, then use Goal Seek.)

5. You want to modify the spreadsheet to make it easier to use.

    a. Include relevant comments describing how the price per ticket and security expense are calculated.

    b. You want to show the financial team remembers how certain things are calculated in the break-even analysis. Insert a comment explaining how the IF statement is used to calculate the Cost of Staff.

Dr. William Gardner's Dental Office

Marketing Analysis

EXCEL WORKING CASE: BEGINNING LEVEL

Submission Instructions Complete Case 12 in Excel. Answer the questions at the end of this case and insert the answers on an Answer Sheet within the Case 12 Excel spreadsheet. Ask your instructor for submission instructions.

Preview You are the marketing manager for Dr. Gardner's Dental Office. You need a new marketing campaign for two of the dental services that the office provides. You decide to create a spreadsheet for the services the dental office provides with the hope of discovering which services you want to focus on in your next ad campaign.

Skill Set

Format spreadsheet
Absolute reference
Sum, maximum, minimum functions
Date function
Goal seek (question at end of case)
If function
Vlookup table
AutoFilter
Center merge
Chart (question at end of case)

Background Dr. William Gardner's Dental Office has three different office locations. Each location offers a variety of dental services, and you want to know which services are most popular in each of the offices. This is why you want to create a spreadsheet in Excel. You also want to know which service brings in the most revenue at each office, and from this information, you will focus your ad campaign on two services.

▶ CASE ANALYSIS

Output Requirements

Create a spreadsheet that you can use to keep track of services rendered for each of his three offices. For each office, you need to see the total amount billed for each of the various dental services, as well as the total amount and average amount of each service within each office, and the total amount earned from all three of the offices.

Input Requirements

Table 12.1 provides information on services rendered.

Table 12.2 shows the price for each service and the percentage of insurance coverage. Create the table in your spreadsheet. Use the table as a Vlookup table when you create the formula to calculate the amount owed by insurance.

Processing Requirements

Table 12.3 shows the required formulas to be implemented in the spreadsheet application.

Table 12.1 Number of Services Rendered

Service	Office 1	Office 2	Office 3
Bridge	8	18	23
Cavity fill	12	22	7
Dentures	4	7	6
Extractions	6	9	3
Replace fillings	2	6	11
Teeth cleaning	8	3	17
Teeth whitening	9	4	4
Tooth implant	10	8	5

Table 12.2 Service Prices and Insurance (Assumption Box)

Type of Service	Price per Treatment ($)	Percentage of Insurance Coverage
Bridge	300	50
Cavity fill	200	20
Dentures	2,300	60
Extraction	250	55
Replace fillings	350	35
Teeth cleaning	150	30
Teeth whitening	800	0
Tooth implant	1,200	45

Table 12.3 Revenue Formulas

Costs and Revenues	Formula
Total revenue of services (each office)	Service ∗ Price per treatment (assumption box)
Billed to insurance	(Vlookup table for percentage of insurance coverage) ° Total sales for services
Billed to patient	Total amount for service − Insurance coverage
Total revenue for all three offices	(Total sales office 1) + (Total sales office 2) + (Total sales office 3)

▶ DESIGN AND IMPLEMENTATION

Figure 12.1 shows the desired rectangular worksheet layout of the application. Note that the three dentist office service logs are arranged in the same way. The three service logs compose the entire weekly service log. Note the rectangular layout and position of the assumptions area.

Documentation

Type the four column headings for the service log. Type the row labels for Office 1; you can copy them to create the Office 2 and Office 3 row labels. Type the column headings and row labels for the assumption area. Make sure you include a relevant title for the weekly service log; use a Date function to show the current date below the title. Apply the relevant value-added features to improve the readability of the text, such as indenting the service type labels, using line borders and shading, and varying font size appropriately. Name the worksheet Service Log.

Input Area

Use Table 12.1 as your guide to type the number of services rendered in Table 12.2 to help you enter the parameter values in the Assumptions area. Make sure you use an appropriate format for the numbers.

Processing Area

Use Table 12.3 to guide your entering of the formulas. An efficient way to enter the formulas is to first enter the Office 1 formulas, making sure you use cell references for the parameter values in the formulas and the appropriate absolute cell addressing for those cell references. Use the Audit Formulas tool to verify that you have correctly entered the formulas for Office 1. You can then copy the formulas to Office 2 and Office 3. Make sure you apply an appropriate format to the numbers.

Dr. William Gardner's Dental Office Weekly Service Log Date				
	Total Services	Total Revenue for Service	Billed to Insurance	Billed to Patient
Office 1				
Bridge	8			
Cavity fill	12			
Dentures	4			
Extractions	6			
Replace Fillings	2			
Teeth Cleaning	8			
Teeth Whitening	9			
Tooth Implant	10			
Total Revenue				
Office 2				
Bridge	18			
Cavity fill	22			
Dentures	7			
Extractions	9			
Replace Fillings	6			
Teeth Cleaning	3			
Teeth Whitening	4			
Tooth Implant	8			
Total Revenue				
Office 3				
Bridge	23			
Cavity fill	7			
Dentures	6			
Extractions	3			
Replace Fillings	11			
Teeth Cleaning	17			
Teeth Whitening	4			
Tooth Implant	5			
Total Revenue				
Total Revenue for 3 offices				

Figure 12.1 Weekly Service Log Layout

▶ USING THE SPREADSHEET APPLICATION

As the marketing manager, you want to use the application to think about which services to include in a new marketing campaign. On a new worksheet in the same workbook create another worksheet, named AnswerSheet, for answering the following questions. Where appropriate, create a formula to calculate the correct answer. Before answering each question, reset the Break-Even Analysis worksheet to its original values.

1. As the marketing analyst, you need to get an idea of how well the three dentist offices perform on key performance indicators.

   a. What is the total combined revenue for all three offices?

   b. What is the total revenue for each of the eight services?

   c. Which service brings in the most overall revenue?

   d. Which service brings in the least overall revenue?

   e. Which office is making the most money on services?

   f. What is the overall total average amount billed to the clients?

2. You need to visualize the revenues for each service and each dentist office.

   a. Compare the revenues for each service for each of the three offices. Use a stacked-column chart. Make sure to include a title, and format the y-axis to show the revenue in thousands. Move the chart to a new worksheet and rename the worksheet tab Service Chart. Viewing the chart, what revenue patterns across services do you see? Across the three offices?

   b. Determine the percentage of total sales for Office 3 for each of the eight services. Use a pie chart. Make sure to include a title and format the data labels appropriately. Move the pie chart onto a new worksheet and rename the worksheet tab Office 3 Pie Chart.

3. You are discussing with Dr. Gardner the assumptions of how the number of treatments (customers) for each of the eight services relate to the price of each service.

   a. What would be the combined overall total revenue from all three offices if the Cavity Fill service was increased to $300, but the number of Cavity fills in each of the three offices was reduced by 5% because of the increased price. Is the total revenue higher or lower?

   b. What would be combined overall total revenue from all three offices if the Teeth Cleaning and the Teeth Whitening services were reduced to $125 and $750 respectively?

4. You want to explore several what-if scenarios. Use the Goal Seek tool to calculate the answers to the following questions.

   a. Dr. Gardner would like to increase total revenue to $122,000. To reach this goal, how much does he need to charge for the Tooth Implant service, assuming there are no changes in the number of customers (treatments). Is this a reasonable price to charge?

b. The cost of dental insurance is increasing. Assume that the Percentage of Insurance Coverage for the Dentures services changes from the current 60% to 50%. What should Dr. Gardner charge for the Dentures service so that the amount billed to patients is about the same as before?

c. You are considering a marketing campaign for Teeth Whitening for Office 1. How many more Teeth Whitening service treatments are needed to reach Office 1 total revenue of $50,000? (Round to the nearest whole number.)

5. You decided to create a marketing campaign for each office. Your budget is determined based on the total sales of each office. If the total sales of an office is more than $40,000, your marketing budget for that office is 5% of the total revenue; if your sales total is below $40,000, you will only have 3% for your marketing budget. Based on the current information, determine each office's marketing budget.

6. You want to modify the spreadsheet to make it easier to use.

a. We would like more customers, but it is unrealistic to expect more than 50 customers for any particular type of service at any of the three offices. As an initial example, create a data validation rule for the Office 1 Bridge service so that no more than 50 can be entered into that cell. (Hint: Use the Data — Validation command.)

b. Include relevant comments for Office 1 describing how Billed to Insurance and Billed to Patient are calculated.

CHAPTER 5

Excel—Intermediate Design Techniques

Up the Hill Bakery
Financial Projections

EXCEL TEACHING CASE: INTERMEDIATE LEVEL

Submission Instructions Complete Case 13 in Excel. Answer the questions at the end of this case and insert the answers on an Answer Sheet within Case 13 Excel spreadsheet. Ask your instructor for submission instructions.

Preview The bakery has hired you as a management consultant. You are going to analyze their financial performance for a possible expansion of their business. You need to create an annual financial projection spreadsheet to better understand the finances of the bakery. You want to research their revenue streams as well as their net profit. You will create a quarterly financial breakdown to review the possibilities of their catering division.

Skill Set

If function
Statistical functions
3-Dimensional workbook
Chart
Format worksheets

Background The owners of the bakery have hired you as a management consultant to analyze their financial performance for a possible expansion of their business. They have kept track of the total monthly sales for five sales categories: bakery items, beverages, breads, breakfast, and lunch. They have also calculated the bakery's average percentage that goes toward the cost of each sales category; this percentage is called Cost of Goods Sold. The bakery also has fixed costs that don't really fluctuate during the year; these fixed costs include the building lease, utilities, salaries, and general administrative costs. The owners of the bakery also give the employees a bonus if their total sales are greater than a certain amount. Currently this bonus amount is $3,000, which is divided up equally every month among the employees.

▶ CASE ANALYSIS

Output Requirements

Create a spreadsheet application showing the quarterly financial projections and annual net profit for the current calendar year. The information for each quarter includes sales, cost of goods sold, fixed expenses including employee salary and bonus expenses, and appropriate totals and other statistics. Each of the four quarters needs to be on a separate worksheet, as shown in Figure 13.1, with consistent formatting across the four worksheets in the workbook. You need to create the totals for each quarter and the annual totals information on a fifth worksheet.

Input Requirements

Table 13.1 shows the total sales of each sales category for January of this year.

Table 13.2 shows the typical Cost of Goods Sold percentages for each sales category. Cost of Goods Sold for each sales category is calculated as the Cost of Goods Sold percentage of sales for that category.

Table 13.1 January Sales

Goods Sold	Total Sales ($)
Beverage	5,500
Bread	8,500
Bakery Items	7,200
Lunch Menu Items	8,400
Breakfast Menu Items	4,500

Table 13.2 Cost of Goods Sold Percentages

Goods Sold	Percentage of Total Sales
Beverage	25%
Bread	15%
Bakery Items	10%
Lunch Menu Items	15%
Breakfast Menu Items	12%

Up the Hill Bakery				
1st Quarter Financial Projections				
Date				
	January	February	March	Total
Sales				
Beverage	$ 5,500.00			
Bread	$ 8,500.00			
Bakery Items	$ 7,200.00			
Lunch Sales	$ 8,400.00			
Breakfast Sales	$ 4,500.00			
Total Sales				
Cost of Good Sold				
Beverage				
Bread				
Bakery Items				
Lunch Sales				
Breakfast Sales				
Total Cost of Good Sold				
Fixed Costs				
Building Lease	$ 2,000			
Utilities	$ 950			
Marketing	$ 1,050			
General Administration	$ 350			
Employee Salaries	$ 11,000			
Bonus Pay Out	XXX			
Total Fixed Costs				
Total Expenses				

st Quarter   2nd Quarter   3rd Quarter   4th Quarter   Annual Sales

Figure 13.1   Worksheet layout for 1st Quarter

Table 13.3 shows the fixed cost for each of the five cost categories. Each of these costs is assumed to be the same value from month to month.

Each employee can earn a bonus. Table 13.4 shows the bonus payout and the bonus sales criterion. The bonus payout is the amount the bakery will pay to the employees if they reach the sales limit, and this bonus is then split among the employees. The bonus sales criterion is the total sales amount that needs to be achieved for employees to receive the bonus.

Table 13.5 shows the assumed percentage increase of monthly sales for each month. The calculation of the sales increase is made with the prior month's sales. For example, February's increase is calculated based on January sales, and March's increase is based on February sales.

Table 13.3 Fixed Costs

Cost Category	Fixed Cost ($)
Building lease	2,000
Utilities	950
Marketing	1,050
General administration	350
Employee salaries	11,000

Table 13.4 Bonus Assumptions

Quarter	Bonus Sales criterion
1st Quarter	$34,500
2nd Quarter	$36,000
3rd Quarter	$37,500
4th Quarter	$40,000

Table 13.5 Monthly Sales Percentage Change

Month	Increase in Sales from Previous Month (%)
February	1%
March	1.2%
April	2%
May	1%
June	2.5%
July	1%
August	2%
September	0%
October	1%
November	3%
December	4%

Processing Requirements

Quartely Worksheets:

Table 13.6 shows the required formulas to be implemented in the spreadsheet application.

Before you begin, you must group your sheets. To group the worksheets, hold the shift key down and select each of the four quarterly worksheet tabs to define a three-dimensional space. The worksheet tab labels dim to indicate which worksheets have been grouped. To ungroup the worksheets, simply click on any one of the worksheet tabs.

Table 13.7 shows the formulas for the quarterly financial projections for the current calendar year.

Annual Sales Worksheets:

1. Create a new sheet and name it Annual Sales. Copy the first column content from the first-quarter worksheet to the Annual Sales Sheet. Do not include the assumption box.

2. Use the 3-D formula to gather the totals for each category from each of the quarterly worksheets. Total Sales for beverages is =SUM('1st Quarter:4th Quarter'!E6). Use Figure 13.2 as a guide to complete the Annual Sales summary.

3. Show your formulas. On the Formula bar, within the formula auditing group, select Show formulas. Check your work to make sure your formulas are correct.

Table 13.6 Financial Projection Formulas

Category	Formulas	Comments
**Group your sheets		
Total sales	Sum function	Sum function for all sales categories (beverage, bread, bakery items, lunch, and breakfast sales)
Building Lease	Cell Reference from the fixed cost assumption box	
Cost of Goods sold (CGS)	Total sales of that sales category * CGS percentage	CGS is located in the assumption box.
Total cost of goods sold	Sum function	Sum function for all CGS sales categories (beverage, bread, bakery items, lunch, and breakfast sales)
Fixed costs	Enter a cell reference from the assumption box for each fixed costs	
Bonus payout	If statement based on bonus sales criterion Logical test: Total sales > bonus sales goal True: Bonus False: "" [double quotes]	Insert double quotes so the cell is blank. You are creating a statistical formula that needs the false statement to be blank instead of 0.
Total fixed costs	Sum function	Sum function for all categories under fixed costs
Total expenses	Total fixed costs + total cost of goods sold	
Net income	Total sales − total expenses	
Taxes	Net income * 35%	
Net profit	Net income taxes	
Total	Summation	Summation of the 3 months for each line item
February:	January beverage sales * (1 + Percentage increase for February)	
March:	February beverage sales * (1 + Percentage increase for March)	
** ungroup your sheets		

Table 13.7 Financial Projection Formulas for 3-D Worksheet

Category	Prior Month Formula
April numbers in 2nd quarter	March beverage sales (3D cell reference) * (1 + percentage increase for April)
July numbers in 3rd quarter	June beverage sales (3D cell reference) * (1 + percentage increase for July)
October numbers in 4th quarter	September beverage sales (3D cell reference) * (1 + percentage increase for July)

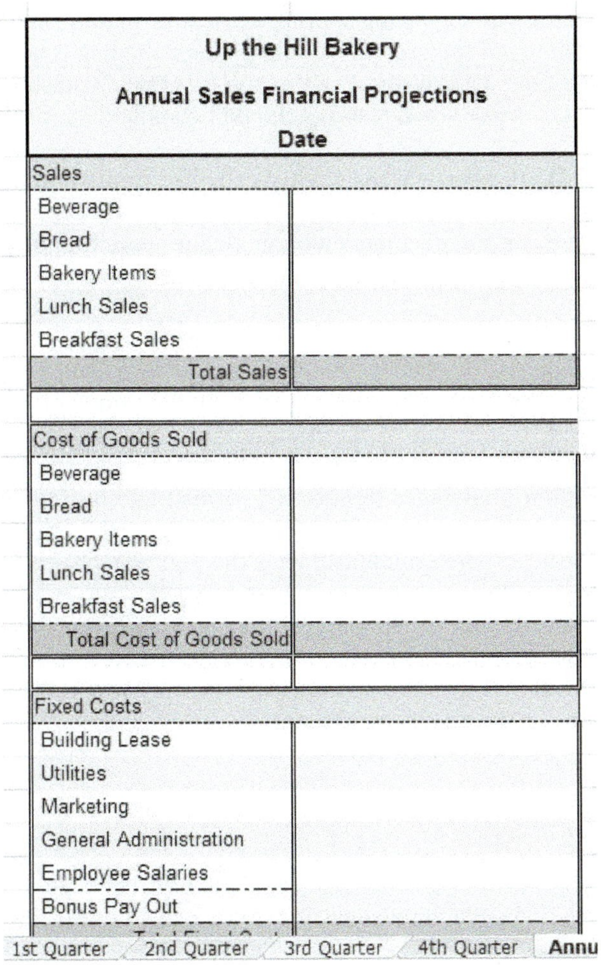

Up the Hill Bakery	
Annual Sales Financial Projections	
Date	
Sales	
Beverage	
Bread	
Bakery Items	
Lunch Sales	
Breakfast Sales	
Total Sales	
Cost of Goods Sold	
Beverage	
Bread	
Bakery Items	
Lunch Sales	
Breakfast Sales	
Total Cost of Goods Sold	
Fixed Costs	
Building Lease	
Utilities	
Marketing	
General Administration	
Employee Salaries	
Bonus Pay Out	

1st Quarter / 2nd Quarter / 3rd Quarter / 4th Quarter / **Annu**

Figure 13.2 Annual Sales Layout

▶ DESIGN AND IMPLEMENTATION

Figure 13.1 shows the layout of the first quarter worksheet; the layouts of the second, third, and fourth quarter worksheets in the workbook are the same, except for appropriate modifications of column headings and the assumptions row labels and values.

Documentation

Design Principle

Quarterly Worksheets—In Figure 13.1, the various titles, row labels, and column headings orient the user to the meaning of the various numeric values to be shown on the worksheet. Note how the labels for the sales, cost of goods sold, fixed costs, and totals are grouped together; applying appropriate text formatting and indentation would increase the readability of the groupings' labels. Color shading is a useful technique for differentiating the four worksheets. Each of the quarterly worksheets should have an appropriate title. The same visual features should be applied consistently to each of the four worksheets.

Annual Sales Worksheet—Managers typically like to use summary reports, which summarize the detail information from one or more worksheets. A summary report layout is designed using the documentation guidelines common to all worksheets, and the calculations are usually summary statistics such as totals and averages.

Implementation

Quarterly Worksheets—For each of the four worksheets, enter an appropriate title above the months' column headings. Apply the same unique color shading to each of worksheet tabs and to the cells of the Assumptions area. You can consistently apply text formatting and indentation to the four worksheets' row labels by first grouping the worksheets. You then implement the desired formatting and indentation on the first quarter worksheet, and they are applied automatically to the other three worksheets. Ungroup the worksheets when you finish. View the four worksheets to confirm that they are formatted consistently.

Annual Sales Worksheet—Using Figure 13.2 as a guide, create a fifth worksheet in the workbook, positioning it to the right of the fourth quarter worksheet. Enter Annual Sales as the tab label and type the appropriate summary report titles; simply copy the row labels from one of the quarter worksheets.

Input Area

Design Principle

Quarterly Worksheets—The January sales are the only sales input data, as shown in Table 13.1. All of the other input data for this application are parameter values, as show in Tables 13.2 through 13.5. Note how the Assumptions area is designed, grouping the parameters into logical units in each of the four quarter worksheets. Value-added features such as line borders and, especially, numeric formatting improve the readability of the input areas.

Implementation

Quarterly Worksheets—Use the worksheet grouping technique to apply appropriate value-added features to the input areas of the four quarterly worksheets.

Processing Area

Design Principle

Quarterly Worksheets—The layout of the quarterly worksheets is arranged as a rectangle, with columns of calculations corresponding to each of the three months in the quarter, along with two columns of statistics calculations, the total for each of the row line items. The Assumptions area is also laid out in a rectangle; many of the formulas use these parameter values. Note that the layout is exactly the same in the four quarterly worksheets, conceptually forming a three-dimensional cube. The formulas must be correct; otherwise the spreadsheet application will calculate incorrect answers and be of little value to the user. After you create or copy a formula, you should check to make sure the answer is correct. All the numbers should be formatted consistently to improve readability.

Implementation

Quarterly Worksheets—Begin by entering the formulas for January. You can then use the worksheet grouping technique to enter many of the other formulas for the quarterly worksheets. Make sure you correctly use the parameter cell addresses in formulas rather than typing the numeric value into the formula. Finally, enter the formulas in the Annual Sales worksheet; make sure you correctly use 3-D formulas. Use the Audit Formulas tool to verify that you have entered all the formulas correctly. Make sure you think about whether or not the formulas are calculating appropriate values. Format the numbers using the Accounting format with zero decimals.

▷ USING THE SPREADSHEET APPLICATION

As the management consultant to Jack and Susan, you can use the spreadsheet application to analyze the bakery's projected revenues and answer a variety of what-if questions in order to make recommendations regarding a possible expansion of the bakery's catering business. To answer the following questions, create another worksheet named Answer-Sheet and position it to the right of the Annual Sales worksheet. Where appropriate, create a formula to calculate the correct answer. Before answering each question, reset the parameter values to their original values.

1. Refer to the summary report on the projected Annual Sales worksheet and answer the following questions.
    a. Bakery Items account for what percentage of total projected sales?
    b. Bakery Items account for what percentage of Total Cost of Goods Sold?
    c. Which Fixed Cost item accounts for the highest percentage of Total Fixed Costs?
2. You want to investigate how changing assumptions about costs and monthly sales increases would affect projected net profit.
    a. Looking at the First Quarter worksheet, if the assumed Cost of Goods Sold for Bread and Bakery Items are changed to 13% and 9%, respectively, and the February and March sales increase percentages are changed to 1.3% and 1.5%, respectively, what are the projected Total Sales, Total Expenses, and Net Income for the first quarter? For the year? Are these significant sales and income increases?
    b. Think about the third and fourth quarters. If the assumed Marketing fixed cost is changed to $1,200 for the two quarters and the assumed monthly sales increase

percentages are increased 0.5% for each of the six months, what are the Total Sales, Total Expenses, and Net Income for the third quarter? For the fourth quarter? For the year? Are these significant sales and income increases?

3. You want to investigate how changes in the bakery's bonus policy affect revenues and expenses.

    a. Looking at the first quarter, what is the Total Bonus Pay Out if the assumed Bonus Sales Goal is changed to $36,000 and the assumed Bonus Pay is changed to $3,500? How much does Total Fixed Costs change for the first quarter? Is this desirable from the bakery's point of view?

    b. Looking at the second quarter, you want to explore both increasing bonuses and reducing costs. Assume that the Cost of Goods Sold percentages for the Bread and Bakery Items are changed to 13% and 9%, respectively, and the Bonus Sales Goal is changed to $30,000. What are the changes for Total Cost of Goods Sold and Net Income for the second quarter? Do changes in these assumptions make a big difference from the bakery's point of view? From the employees' point of view?

    c. Looking at the third quarter, if the bakery could improve sales by assuming a sales increase percentage for July of 2%, August of 4%, and September of 2%, what is the change in the total Bonus Pay Out for the quarter?

4. You want to remember how certain things are calculated in the application. Insert a comment in the Total Sales on the Annual Sales worksheet describing the 3-D formula. Also insert a comment in February's Beverage cell describing the sales projection formula.

5. You want to visualize the bakery's financial projections in a variety of ways.

    a. Show how each of the five sales items contributes to total sales for the year. Create a 3-D pie chart using Annual Sales for Beverage, Bread, Bakery Items, Breakfast Sales, and Lunch Sales. Make sure you use value-added features such as a title, color scheme, and comments to improve the chart's usefulness. Save the chart as a separate worksheet named Annual Sales Chart and position it to the right of the Annual Sales worksheet. Looking at the pie chart, which category has the lowest sales? Bread sales accounts for what percentage of sales?

    b. You want to visualize the trend of Total Sales and Total Expenses over the year's 12 months. Create an appropriate line chart showing months along the horizontal axis. You will first need to create the two data series and the labels series on the AnswerSheet worksheet. Make sure you apply helpful value-added features to the chart. Save the chart as a separate worksheet named Projection Trends Chart and position it to the right of the Bonus Pay Out Chart worksheet. Looking at the chart, is there a desirable trend from the bakery's point of view?

6. As the bakery's management consultant, you want to make recommendations based on changing certain assumptions to reach particular net profit goals. Use the Goal Seek tool (Data — What-if) to calculate the answers to the following questions.

   a. The bakery would like to see a net profit for the first quarter of $28,000. What Monthly Sales Increase percentage for March is needed to reach that goal?

   b. The bakery wants a net profit for the second quarter of $28,000. Can the goal be reached by changing the Bonus Pay for the quarter?

7. Jack and Susan would really like to expand the bakery's business at least 5% over the next year. To increase the year's net profit by at least 5%, they could do a combination of things, such as try to improve monthly sales, decrease cost of goods sold, decrease overall fixed costs, or some combination and at the same time improve the bonus pay for employees. Based on your use of the spreadsheet application, what recommendation(s) would you give Jack and Susan?

JB Bike Rental

Sales Analysis

EXCEL WORKING CASE: INTERMEDIATE LEVEL

Submission Instructions Complete Case 14 in Excel. Answer the questions at the end of this case and insert the answers on an Answer Sheet within Case 14 Excel spreadsheet. Ask your instructor for submission instructions.

Preview Josh Blade owns JB Bike Rental. He operates three stores in the San Diego area. He wants you, his store manager, to create a spreadsheet application for his daily sales of all three stores. Josh wants you to incorporate an easy way to change rental prices and hourly rental discount rates depending on seasonal demand. You need to create the information for each store on a separate worksheet within one workbook, as well as a fourth worksheet that includes a summary of the total sales information for each of the stores.

Skill Set

If function
Statistical functions
3-Dimensional workbook
Chart
Format worksheets

Background Josh Blade owns JB Bike Rental, which rents various types of bikes on an hourly basis. Josh operates three stores in the San Diego area: Downtown, Pacific Beach, and Oceanside. He wants you to create a spreadsheet depicting the bike rentals during the day at each store. You are to calculate the total rental hours for each type of bike and the total sales from the rentals. The owner usually gives a 10% discount to customers if they rent for more than 3 hours, although he sometimes increases or decreases the discount depending on the season. Josh also changes the hourly rental rate depending on the season. Because he frequently changes the discount rate and the hourly bike rental rate, he wants you to design a spreadsheet application that is flexible and easy to use.

► CASE ANALYSIS

Output Requirements

Create a spreadsheet application that shows JB Bike Rental's daily sales report for each of the three stores and a worksheet that shows a summary report of all three stores. Each store location should have its own worksheet within the workbook. Figures 14.1 and 14.2 show a desired layout for the daily sales report and the summary report.

Input Requirements

The customers' names, the type of bike rented, and the rental hours are provided in the student file. Table 14.1 shows the discount information for each store.

Processing Requirements

1. Begin by naming the sheets. Name sheet 1 Downtown, sheet 2 Pacific Beach, and sheet 3 Oceanside.

2. Group your sheets by holding your shift key down and selecting each of the three worksheet tabs to define a three-dimensional space.
   Table 14.2 shows the required formulas to be implemented in the spreadsheet application.

► DESIGN AND IMPLEMENTATION

Use the Case specifications to complete the spreadsheet application. Use the three-dimensional space technique to implement features for all three daily sales report worksheets where appropriate.

Documentation

The Three Location Worksheets

View each of the three location worksheets and notice that they have a different text for the title, but they have the same layout for the title and column headings, the daily total and average rows, the Rental Rates table, and the Discount table; see Figure 14.1 for the layout. First, enter an appropriate name for each of the three worksheet tabs, then group the three worksheets and apply appropriate text formatting and alignment,

Table 14.1 Discount Information

Store	Discount Hour	Discount Amount (%)
Downtown	3	10
Pacific Beach	4	12
Oceanside	3.5	5

JB Bike Rental Downtown

Date

Name	Bike Type	Rental Hours	Total Rental Amount	Total Rental Amount w/discount
Ron Donahue	Cruiser	4		
Julia Beeson	Cruiser	4		
Phyllis DeBlanche	Cruiser	3		
Thomas Arnold	Cruiser	4		
Rita Weiss	Cruiser	7		
Thomas Shess	Mountain	2		
Don Braunagel	Mountain	4		
Laura Byrd	Mountain	1		
Cathy Clarde	Mountain	3		
Kevin Cox	Mountain	4		
Kathleen Gurnett	Mountain	2		
Margie Farnsworth	Hybrid	5		
Thomas Arnold	Hybrid	1		
Diane Nelson	Professional	3		
Michael Mode	Professional	3		
Larry Edwards	Professional	2		
Daily Total				
Daily Average				

Rental Rates		
Cruiser	$	10.00
Hybrid	$	12.00
Mountain	$	14.00
Professional	$	16.00

Discount	
Discount Hour	3
Discount Amount	10%

Downtown Pacific Beach Ocean Side Summary AnswerSheet

Figure 14.1 Daily Sales Report Layout

Summary of Total Daily Sales 7/10/2012			
Store Location	Total Rental Hours	Total Rental Amount	Total Rental Amount w/Discount
Downtown	0	$ -	$ -
Pacific Beach	45	$ 594.00	$ 559.20
Ocean Side	68	$ 883.00	$ 847.95
Total	113	$ 1,477.00	$ 1,407.15

Figure 14.2 Summary Report Layout

Table 14.2 Spreadsheet Formulas

** Group Sheets Total Rental Amount	vlookup function based on the rental rates assumption box

Total Rental Amount with
  Discount
	IF Statement
	  Logical Test: Hours > = Discount Hour
	  True: Total Rental Amount * (1 - Discount Amount)
	  False: Total Rental Amount

Daily Total, Daily Average	Sum Function, Average Function
*Ungroup Sheets	Right click on a sheet and select ungroup sheets

Total Rental Hours, Total
  Rental Amount and Total
  Rental Amount with Discount
	Use a 3-D Formula to calculate the total hours for each
	  location i.e. =Downtown!D21

Totals	Sum Function

numeric formatting, and color shading. Make sure you merge cells to center the title and use the Date function to show the current date on the row beneath the title. Ungroup the worksheets when you finish.

Summary Worksheet

Figure 14.2 shows the desired layout of the summary report. Create a new worksheet named Summary and then use Figure 14.2 as your guide to enter the title, date function, column headings, and row labels. Apply all the relevant value-added features to the column headings and row labels to improve the readability of the report. Make sure you use the Date function to show the current date below the title.

Input Area

Three Location Worksheets shown in Figure 14.1, each of the three location worksheets has two input areas: the customer rental data and the rental rate and discount assumptions. The input data is provided to you; however, you should use the worksheet grouping technique to apply desired text and numeric formatting, especially to the numeric parameter values.

Processing Area

The Three Location Worksheets

Use Table 14.2 as your guide for entering the formulas. You should take advantage of the 3-D structure of the combined three worksheets to enter the formulas. First, group the three worksheets, then enter the two formulas for the first customer, making sure you use absolute cell addressing when referencing the parameter cells in the formulas. Then copy the formulas to the remaining customers. Make sure you create total and average formulas as well and apply the Accounting format with two decimals to the numbers. Ungroup the worksheets when you are finished, but make sure you use the Audit Formulas tool to verify that the formulas are correct on each of the three worksheets.

Summary Worksheet

Using Table 14.2 as your guide, enter the appropriate 3-D formulas and then verify that the formulas are correct. Apply the Accounting format with two decimals to the numbers.

▷ USING THE SPREADSHEET APPLICATION

As the store manager for JB Bike Rental, you want to see how each store performed that day and explore how different rental and discount rates would have changed daily sales amounts. On a new worksheet in the same workbook, create a fifth worksheet, named AnswerSheet, for answering the following questions. Where appropriate, create a formula to calculate the correct answer. Before answering each question, make sure all the parameter values are returned to the given values from the case.

1. You want to get an idea of how each location performed that day.

   a. Looking at the Downtown location, how much did each customer spend, on average? At the Pacific Beach location? At the Oceanside location?

   b. Looking at the Downtown location, what type of bike is the most profitable (after discount)? At the Pacific Beach location? At the Oceanside location? (Hint: Use the Pivot Table feature if you are familiar on how to use it.)

2. You view the summary report to get an idea of the overall performance of the business for that day

   a. Name the stores in order from the store that generated the most income to the store that generated the least income.

   b. How much was allowed for discounts that day?

3. You want to consider how changing rental rates would have affected the daily sales, or Total Rental Amount with discount.

   a. For the Pacific Beach location, how much would the daily sales change if the rental rate for both Mountain and Professional bikes were $15? Is this amount of change worth considering?

   b. For the Oceanside location, how much would the daily sales change if the rental rate for Cruiser and Hybrid bikes were each increased by $1?

4. You want to consider how changing the discounts would have affected the daily sales, or Total Rental Amount with discount.

   a. What would be the total sales for all three stores if you changed the discount hour minimum to five hours for all three locations?

   b. What would be the total sales for all three stores if you changed the discount hour minimum to five hours and the discount amount changed to 12%? Would this be a reasonable decision to make?

5. Josh Blade, the owner, would like to see each location have daily sales, or Total Rental Amount with discount, of at least $600. Use the Goal Seek tool to help answer the following questions.

   a. For the Pacific Beach location, what would the rental rate for Professional bikes have to be to meet that goal? Is this a reasonable price increase?

   b. For the Downtown location, what would the rental rate for Mountain bikes have to be to meet that goal? For the Cruiser bikes? Which would be the better choice?

6. You want to visually compare the store locations based on both the total rental amount and the total rental amount with discount. On the Summary worksheet, create a column chart showing the comparison. Add value to the chart with a title, legend, x-axis and y-axis titles, y-axis numeric formatting, and appropriate chart area formatting features. Position the chart underneath the summary report.

Torero Tennis Team

Athletics Statistics

EXCEL WORKING CASE: INTERMEDIATE LEVEL

Submission Instructions Complete Case 15 in Excel. Answer the questions at the end of this case and insert the answers on an answer sheet within Case 15 Excel spreadsheet. Ask your instructor for submission instructions.

Preview The Torero men's tennis team would like to you to create a spreadsheet application for their game statistics. The coach and the team members would like to analyze team's strengths and weaknesses. The coach has recorded game statistics during the first round for each of the players in each of three tournaments. He wants to use the statistics to analyze each player's and whole-team percentages for completed serves, unforced errors, serve returns, and other performance criteria. The coach wants you to finish the spreadsheet he has started. When you have completed this spreadsheet, the coach can use this information to design a better practice and tennis drills for his team.

Skill Set

If function
Statistical functions
3-Dimensional workbook
Chart
Format worksheets

Background The Torero tennis team consists of six players who have played three tournaments this year: West Conference, San Diego Open, and Spring Classic. The team's coach wants to analyze each player's strengths and weakness, including serves, serve returns, volleys, and unforced errors. The coach has recorded game statistics during the first round for each of the six players in each of the three tournaments. In the first round of the tournaments each player played a three-set match (three sets consists of a number of games; the first player to win six games wins the set and the first player to win three sets wins the match). The coach wants to see how many games each player won within the three sets and how many serves they were able to complete, as well as how many returns, in-play hits, and unforced errors each player had.

The coach wants to calculate the performance percentages for each player in each tournament and calculate a summary of all three tournaments. The coach has created a rewards system for two skill categories: games-won percentage and first-serve percentage. A Most Valuable Player within a category does not have to attend the extra Sunday practice. The coach wants to automatically calculate the Most Valuable Player(s) in each category based on the spreadsheet statistics.

► CASE ANALYSIS

Output Requirements

Create a spreadsheet application showing the performance statistics of each of the six players for the three tournaments. The statistics for each player includes set win or loss, serves, serve returns, in-play hits, and unforced errors. The coach wants to see his players' information for each tournament laid out in the same way on three worksheets, one worksheet for each tournament. The coach also wants a summary report of the three tournaments on a separate worksheet in the application; the summary worksheet also needs to include the calculations for the Most Valuable Player.

Input Requirements

The performance data of each of the players for the West Conference and San Diego Open tournaments have been provided for you in the Case 15 student file. Table 15.1 shows the performance data you need to input for the Spring Classic tournament.

Table 15.2 shows the criteria the coach wants to use initially to calculate the Most Valuable Player(s) for the three tournaments.

Processing Requirements

Three Tournament Worksheets

Table 15.3 shows the required formulas to be implemented in the spreadsheet application.

The three tournament statistics worksheets have the same layout so that you can use the three-dimensional space technique to implement features common to the three tournament statistics worksheets where appropriate, including formatting the text and numbers and entering the various formulas. Group the three sheets before you enter the formulas in Table 15.3.

Summary Worksheet

1. Prepare a Summary sheet for each players total game wins and losses. The summary worksheet should also show the totals for their first, second and double fault serves. Finally this worksheet will show who is the most valuable player for all three tournaments.

2. Insert a new sheet to the right of San Diego Classic sheet. Name sheet Summary. Refer to Figure 15.2 for layout of the summary sheet.

Table 15.1 Performance Data for the Spring Classic Tournament

	Gary Smith	Kevin Shelly	Devin Shelly	Dave Fleming	Renee Rodriquez	Sam Rogers
Set Win/loss	0	0	0	1	1	1
Game Win (3 sets)	9	7	6	19	18	18
Game Loss (3 sets)	18	18	18	8	9	9
Serves						
Aces	2	3	3	5	3	3
1st Serve	21	26	27	34	35	33
2nd Serve	32	34	35	36	33	32
Double Fault	7	7	8	9	6	6
In-play hits						
Down the line returns	31	30	29	32	26	37
Cross court returns	75	82	85	81	78	85
Volleys	25	22	27	26	25	22
Lobs	4	6	4	7	3	9
Unforced errors						
Hit into net	27	32	25	22	24	21
Hit out of bounds	34	35	32	22	24	21
Serve Return						
Hit into net	15	17	14	10	5	8
Hit out of bounds	14	12	10	11	9	6
Down the line returns	50	47	42	58	60	55
Cross court returns	72	73	69	70	87	81

Table 15.2 Most Valuable Player Performance Criteria

Performance	Criterion
MVP Game Win	>67%
Top Server Win	>37%

Table 15.3 Performance Statistics Calculations

Performance Statistic	Formula
Group Sheets	
Total Games, Total Serves, Total Hits, Total Unforced Errors, Total Serve Returns	Sum Function
Team Total	Sum Function
Games Won Percentage per player	Games Won/Total Games
Games Lost Percentage per player	Games Lost/Total Games
Serve and Serve Return Percentages	Aces/Total Serves, 1st Serve/Total Serves
Ungroup Sheets	

3. Calculate the Win Percentage using the 3-D formula. Add all three totals for wins for each player in all three of the tournaments. Then divide by the total games:

$$= \text{SUM ('West Conference:Spring Classic'!B5)} /$$
$$\text{SUM ('West Conference:Spring Classic'!B7)}$$

4. Calculate the Loss percentage Using the 3-D formula Add all three totals for losses for each player in all three of the tournaments. Then divide by the total games:

$$= \text{SUM ('West Conference:Spring Classic'!B6)} /$$
$$\text{SUM ('West Conference:Spring Classic'!B7)}$$

5. Calculate First Serve, Second Serve and Double Fault using the same 3-D technique you used above to solve the first serve and double fault percentages.

6. Calculate MVP (award sheet):

   IF statement

   Logical test: Players Percentage is greater than MVP criteria

   True: "MVP"

   False: "Extra Practice" (use 3-D worksheets in formula)

7. Calculate Top First Serve:

   IF statement

   Logical test: Players Percentage is greater than MVP criteria

   True: "MVP"

   False: "Extra Practice" (use 3-D worksheets in formula)

► DESIGN AND IMPLEMENTATION

The three tournament statistics worksheets have the same layout so that you can use the three-dimensional space technique to implement features common to the three tournament statistics worksheets where appropriate, including formatting the text and numbers and entering the various formulas.

Documentation

The Three Tournament Worksheets

View the tournament statistics worksheets and notice that the title, column headings, and row labels are positioned in the same cells in each of the worksheets. Group the worksheets and, using Figure 15.1 as a guide, apply appropriate text formatting, including merging cells and centering for the title, indenting the row labels in each of the performance categories—Serves, In Play Hits, Unforced Errors, and Serve Returns—and appropriate color shading. Ungroup the worksheets when you finish.

West Conference Date	Gary Smith	Kevin Shelly	Devin Shelly	Dave Fleming	Renee Rodriquez	Sam Rogers	Team Total
Set Win/loss	1	0	1	1	1	0	
Game Win (3 sets)	18	13	18	19	18	12	
Game Loss (3 sets)	9	19	8	10	7	18	
Total Games							
Serves							
Aces	5	2	3	6	2	1	
1st Serve	23	25	26	25	28	30	
2nd Serve	30	40	42	38	35	36	
Double Fault	6	3	5	5	6	6	
Total Serves							
In Play hits							
Down the line returns	34	36	38	40	41	32	
Cross court returns	78	86	80	78	76	62	
Volleys	30	27	25	26	28	29	
Lobs	9	8	7	9	7	5	
Total Hits							
Unforced Errors							
Hit into net	25	34	32	31	31	30	
Hit out of bounds	28	31	29	28	27	27	
Total Unforced Errors							
Serve Return							
Hit into net	11	13	12	10	8	16	

West Conference / SanDiego Open / Spring Classic / Summary / Serving Percentage Chart / AnswerSheet

Figure 15.1 Layout for Tournament Statistics

Documentation

Summary Worksheet
Create a new worksheet, name it Summary, and position it to the right of the Spring Classic worksheet. Use Figure 15.2 as a guide to implement the layout of the Summary report. Also use Figure 15.2 as your guide to implement the Most Valuable Player criteria table. Make sure you create a relevant title and date feature for Summary report along with the appropriate text formatting. Apply an appropriate color for the worksheet tab and apply the same color for cell shading within the worksheet.

Input Area

Using Table 15.1 as a guide, enter the players' data into the appropriate cells in the Spring Classic worksheet.

Tournament Summary							
Date							
	Win (games)	Losses (games)	1st Serves	2nd Serves	Double Fault	MVP	Top 1st Serve
Gary Smith							
Kevin Shelly							
Devin Shelly							
Dave Fleming							
Renee Rodriquez							
Sam Rogers							

Most Valuable Player Criteria		
MVP Game Win Criterion	Greater Than	67%
Top Server Win Criterion	Greater Than	37%

Figure 15.2 Summary Report Layout

Processing Area

The Three Tournament Worksheets

Use Table 15.3 and the instructions following it as your guide for entering the formulas. Again, you can take advantage of the tournament worksheets' 3-D structure to enter all the formulas quickly. First, group the three tournament worksheets, then enter the total formulas and the percentage formulas for Gary Smith, and then copy those formulas to the five other players. Remember also to create the Team Total formulas. Format the numeric cells and percentage signs where needed. Ungroup the worksheets when you finish, but make sure you use the Audit Formulas tool to verify that the formulas are correct on each of the three worksheets.

Summary Worksheet

Enter the appropriate formulas in the Summary report, using Table 15.3 and the instructions following it as your guide. Use the Audit Formulas tool to verify that the formulas are correct.

▶ USING THE SPREADSHEET APPLICATION

The coach has asked you to evaluate the teams and individual players' strengths and weaknesses. On a new worksheet in the same workbook, create a fifth worksheet, named AnswerSheet, for answering the following questions.

1. The West Conference was the first tournament of the season.
    a. Which player had the most Aces in that tournament?
    b. Which player seemed to be most effective during play (In Play hits)?
    c. Which player needed to most improve in serve return performance?

2. The San Diego Open was played under sunny skies.

   a. Which player most improved his first serve performance between the two tournaments?

   b. Which player most improved his serve return performance between the two tournaments?

   c. In what areas (serves, serve return, and in play hits) did the team, as a whole, improve its performance?

3. The coach wants to evaluate the performance of the team as a whole. Use the Summary worksheet to answer the following questions.

   a. What was the average number of games won among all the players? The average number of losses?

   b. Create a value-added clustered column chart comparing the three serve categories for the six players. Save the chart as a separate worksheet, name the worksheet tab appropriately, and position the worksheet to the right of the Summary worksheet. The coach wants a higher percentage of first serves than second or double-fault serves. Looking at your column chart, which two players need the most help with their serves?

4. What player(s) would have an extra practice if the coach changed the Top Server Win criterion from 37% to 40%?

5. The coach realizes he would like more information in the Summary report. Redesign the Summary report to include the Total Hits and Total Unforced Errors.

CHAPTER 6

Excel—Advanced Design Techniques

Up the Hill Bakery
Building Remodel Proposal

EXCEL TEACHING CASE: ADVANCED LEVEL

Submission Instructions   Complete Case 16 in Excel. Answer the questions at the end of this case and insert the answers on an Answer Sheet in Case 16 Excel spreadsheet. Ask your instructor for submission instructions.

Preview   The owners of Up the Hill Bakery would like to remodel their bakery and create a larger eating area and a larger kitchen. The bakery is currently a 900 square feet, and they would like to add another 400 to 1,100 square feet depending on the cost of materials for the remodel. They have several loan amounts and several different bids for the remodel.

Skill Set

PMT function
Data validation
Solver
Data table
Formula audit
Scenario manager

Background Jack and Susan want you, as the manager of the bakery, to help with their remodeling budget by creating a spreadsheet application they can use to evaluate different combinations of cost and loan amount scenarios for their remodeling project.

Up the Hill Bakery has done very well in the past year, especially the restaurant part of the business. Jack and Susan have decided to build an addition to their bakery and make the dining room larger as well as the kitchen. They would like to change the flooring; install new lighting, tables, and chairs; and install two new ovens. They are on a strict budget and are particularly concerned about the price per square foot for the new addition and the price per square foot for new flooring.

Jack and Susan need you to calculate the total amount of all the remodeling expenses, the percentage of the loan for each expense item, and the price per square foot for the new addition and flooring. They want a visual display showing what their monthly payment would be if they had a 30-year loan and a 15-year loan on a fixed amount of $180,000.

▶ CASE ANALYSIS

Output Requirements

Jack and Susan have some specific information needs for a spreadsheet application to support their remodeling decisions. First, they want a worksheet to view the various costs of the various remodeling components, such as flooring, lighting, and oven, and a total loan amount to fund the remodeling project. Based on the loan amount, they want to see the percentage rate for each of the cost items, as well as the price per square foot for the new addition and the flooring. Figure 16.1 shows a desired layout for this worksheet.

On the second worksheet, Jack and Susan want to see the monthly payments of various loan amounts for both a 30-year 6.5% fixed loan and a 15-year 7.0% fixed loan. They want also to see a table of the monthly payments on different-sized loan amounts for both 30 and 15 years. Figure 16.2 shows a desired layout for this worksheet.

Finally, Jack and Susan want an easy-to-use feature to let them ask what-if questions. Using Solver and Scenario Manager, they can evaluate different combinations, or scenarios, of costs for lighting, flooring, and furniture, to immediately see the change in the loan amount. They can also consider various combinations of expanding the bakery's square footage and the likely costs. Worksheets showing the results of these what-if scenarios are created automatically.

Input Requirements

Table 16.1 shows the initial estimated square footage for the addition and the estimates for each of the seven components of the remodel. Jack and Susan want to be able to modify their initial estimates but want to avoid entering unrealistic estimates, for example, negative numbers and really large values.

Jack and Susan do not want to spend more than a certain amount for restructuring, flooring, and lighting. Table 16.2 shows the spending parameters.

Bakery's Remodel of Existing Space		
Date		

Square feet		600

Dollar Amount for Remodel		
Addition	$	130,600
Flooring	$	9,500
Lighting	$	9,200
Tables	$	7,100
Chairs	$	4,300
New Oven	$	7,500
Wood-fired Oven	$	11,800
Total Loan Amount		

Price Per Square Foot	
Addition	
Flooring	

Percentage Cost of Remodel	
Addition	
Flooring	
Lighting	
Tables	
Chairs	
New Oven	
Wood-fired Oven	

Figure 16.1   Remodel Worksheet Layout

Processing Requirements

The required formulas for the application are to calculate the remodeling costs and to calculate the cost of borrowing the funds needed for the project: the loan costs. Table 16.3 shows the required formulas to calculate the various remodeling costs. Table 16.4 shows the loan cost formulas and parameter values that will be used to evaluate different remodeling scenarios.

Bakery's Remodel of Existing Space

Loan Amount/ Monthly Payments				One Variable Data Table for Various Loan Amounts		
Amount	30 Years	15 Years		Loan Amount	30 Years	15 Years
$ 180,000	XXX	XXX		$ 185,000	XXX	XXX
				$ 190,000	XXX	XXX
				$ 195,000	XXX	XXX
Loan Information				$ 200,000	XXX	XXX
Years	Rate			$ 205,000	XXX	XXX
30	6.5%			$ 210,000	XXX	XXX
15	5%			$ 215,000	XXX	XXX
				$ 220,000	XXX	XXX

Figure 16.2 Loan Worksheet Layout

Table 16.1 Square Footage and Estimated Costs

Square feet	600
Feature	Cost
Restructure add-on	$130,600
Flooring	$ 9,500
Lighting	$ 9,200
Tables	$ 7,100
Chairs	$ 4,300
New oven	$ 7,500
Wood-fired oven	$ 11,800

Table 16.2 Cost Constraints

Feature	Cost	Constraints
Addition	$130,600	Less than or equal to $145,000
Flooring	$ 9,500	Less than or equal to $15,000
Lighting	$ 9,200	Less than or equal to $10,000

Table 16.3   Remodel Processing Requirements

Feature	Formula
Total loan amount	Sum Function
Price per sq ft of addition	Dollar amount for addition / square foot
Price per sq ft for flooring	Dollar amount for flooring / square foot
Percentage cost of remodel	Dollar amount of (Remodel Item) / total loan amount

Table 16.4   Loan Processing Requirements

Processing Requirement	Formulas and Parameters	Comments
PMT function	Rate = Rate (cell reference) / 12 NPR = Years (cell reference) ∗ 12 PV = Loan Amount (cell reference)	Place a negative sign before the function for the solution to show positive.
One variable Data table	What-if Analysis: Data Table Column input cell is Loan Amount Column Input cell is increments of 5,000 starting with $185,000 and ending with $220,000	Reference cells are: Loan amount, 30-year monthly payment, 15-year monthly payment

To format custom cells for One variable data table headings:

1. Click on the cell that represents the Loan Amount in the Data table.

2. Using Format Cells, create a custom format to replace the number. The Loan Amount cell reference with the words "Loan Amount". Replace the 30 year cell reference to the words "30 year". Replace the 15 year cell reference to the words "15 year payment".

3. Use quotations within your custom format.

4. Create Custom formats for the 30-Year and 15-Year Value Headings.

► DESIGN AND IMPLEMENTATION

This spreadsheet application has two worksheets, each designed for a particular information need: first, to calculate the remodeling costs, and second, to calculate the loan costs. Two additional worksheets are created automatically using Solver and Scenario Manager to evaluate different remodel-loan scenarios. You want to design the worksheets for readability and the flexibility to create multiple scenarios needed to make the correct decisions.

Documentation: Remodel Worksheet

Design Principle

A worksheet should be designed with visual features to improve the overall readability of the information shown. Well-designed titles, headings and labels, date, color scheme, and numeric formatting are important design features of every worksheet.

Implementation

Using Figure 16.1 as your guide, apply appropriate value-added features to the title, section headings, and row labels.

Input Area: Remodel Worksheet

Design Principle

Wherever the user needs to enter or change the value of a cell in a worksheet, that cell should be designed to remind the user it is an input cell and to prevent inaccurate data from being entered. You can use Excel's Data Validation feature to set upper and lower limits for numeric cells as well as reminder and error messages for the user. Each interactive input cell should be formatted appropriately so the user can quickly verify whether the value is reasonable. Figure 16.3 shows an example of a data validation message.

Implementation

Use the Data Validation command to check for input errors for the Addition, Flooring, and Lighting components; Table 16.2 shows the input constraints. Make sure you enter appropriate input and error messages for those input cells.

Processing Area: Remodel Worksheet

Design Principle

Whenever you enter a formula into a spreadsheet, you should verify that the formula is correct. You can use the Formula Auditing toolbar to quickly verify, visually, whether the correct cell references are used in the formula.

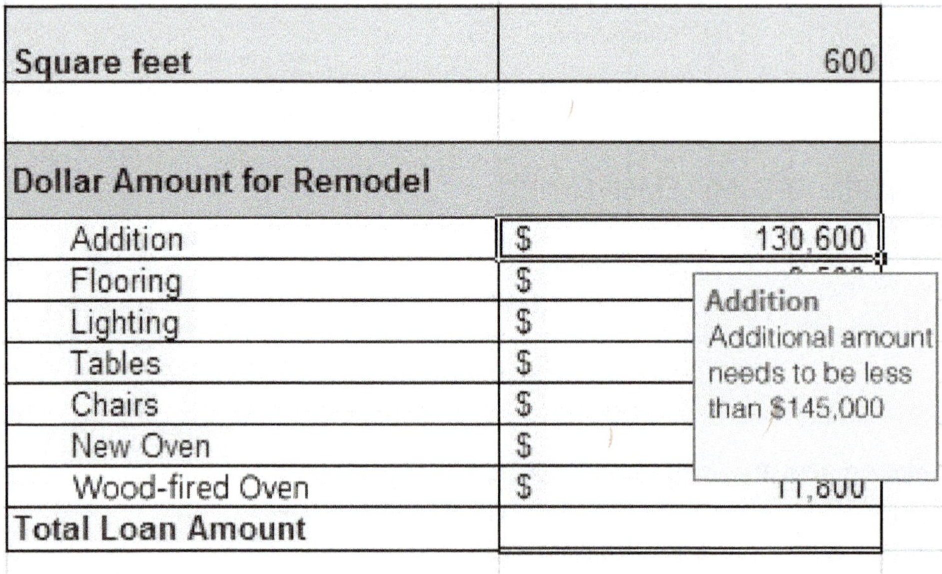

Square feet		600
Dollar Amount for Remodel		
Addition	$	130,600
Flooring	$	
Lighting	$	
Tables	$	
Chairs	$	
New Oven	$	
Wood-fired Oven	$	11,800
Total Loan Amount		

Addition
Additional amount needs to be less than $145,000

Figure 16.3 Data Validation Input Message

Implementation

Using Table 16.3 as your guide, enter the required formulas. Note the matching vertical layout of the input cells and the processing cells; you can take advantage of this by using absolute cell addressing to copy the Percentage Cost of Remodel formulas. Use the Formula Auditing toolbar to verify the formulas by tracing precedent and dependent cells.

Documentation: Loan Worksheet

Remember, as in the Remodel worksheet, to apply appropriate text formatting to the various headings to help the user understand the worksheet's layout. Use Figure 16.2 as your guide.

Input Area: Loan Worksheet

There are five input cells in the worksheet: the loan amount, the values of the two loan periods (30 years and 15 years), and the two loan rates (6.5% and 7%). Enter the loan periods and respective rates, formatting the cells appropriately. The value of the loan amount is calculated on the Remodel worksheet. For the purposes of this case, manually enter the loan amount in this Loan worksheet. Apply color shading to the five cells to remind the user that these are interactive input cells.

Processing Area: Loan Worksheet

Design Principle

An important managerial use of spreadsheet applications is what-if analysis, a process of changing the values of one or more input cells to see how those changes affect the outcome of one or more formulas. A user can use Excel's data table feature to automatically change the values of an input cell and see in a table how those changes affect one or more formulas. Data tables provide a quick and easy way to calculate multiple what-if questions and to view the results of all of the different variations together for easy comparison.

Implementation

First, enter the formulas to calculate the 30-year and 15-year monthly payments, using Table 16.4 as your guide. Beneath the Data Table for Various Loan Amounts heading, create a data table showing the monthly payments for a 30-year loan and for a 15-year loan for loan amounts of $185,000 to $220,000 in increments of $5,000. Refer to Table 16.4 for customizing the column headings of the data table. Make sure you appropriately format the values in the table.

Solver Worksheet

Design Principle

A variation of what-if analysis is to use Excel's Solver tool to search for the best, or optimum, value of a formula by changing the value of one or more input cells, but only within certain limits, or constraints. Solver will automatically show the answer and supporting information on a new worksheet.

For example, Jack and Susan are considering increasing their loan amount from $180,000 to $200,000. They want to use Solver to solve for the $200,000 loan increases, but they want to stay within certain spending limits, or constraints, as shown in Table 16.2. Solver will produce an answer report, shown in Figure 16.4, of a suggested summary of how they could allocate the increase of the loan.

Implementation

Using the Solver tool, enter the desired value of the loan amount (the objective cell), the three input cells (the variable cells), and the three constraints shown in Table 16.2. After the result is calculated, the Solver Results dialog box is shown; select Answer Report to show the report automatically on new worksheet. Name this worksheet Solver and position it to the right of the Loan worksheet.

Scenario Manager Worksheet

Design Principle

A handy way to keep track of scenarios and to compare them in a report is to use the Scenario Manager tool. For example, Jack and Susan initially are considering a 600 square foot expansion with assumed costs for the seven components of the remodel (as shown in Table 16.1); this scenario results in a certain price per square foot for the addition and flooring and a total amount they will need to borrow. But they are also

Total Loan Amount of $200,00 with Addition, Flooring and Lighting Constraints

Objective Cell (Value Of)

Cell	Name	Original Value	Final Value
B12	Total Loan Amount	$ 180,000	$ 200,000

Variable Cells

Cell	Name	Original Value	Final Value	Integer
B5	Addition	$ 130,600	$ 144,300	Contin
B6	Flooring	$ 9,500	$ 15,000	Contin
B7	Lighting	$ 9,200	$ 10,000	Contin

Constraints

Cell	Name	Cell Value	Formula	Status	Slack
B12	Total Loan Amount	$ 200,000	B12=200000	Binding	0
B5	Addition	$ 144,300	B5<=145000	Not Binding	700
B6	Flooring	$ 15,000	B6<=15000	Binding	0
B7	Lighting	$ 10,000	B7<=10000	Binding	0

Figure 16.4   Solver Worksheet

considering expansions of 700 square feet or 800 square feet, with different assumptions about the costs and subsequently different prices per square foot and loan amounts. These three scenarios, shown in Table 16.5, can be stored in the spreadsheet application and then viewed in a report.

Implementation

Select the Remodel worksheet and then use Scenario Manager to add each of the three scenarios shown in Table 16.5. Make sure you name the scenarios appropriately and enter the correct input, or changing, cell addresses and values for each of the scenarios. When you finish entering the scenarios, you can select Show in Scenario Manager to switch between the scenarios, seeing the results of changing the input cells on the three result cells: price per square foot for the addition and flooring and the total loan amount. Also, select Summary in Scenario Manager to create a scenario report summarizing each of the scenarios in a table that is shown automatically on a new worksheet. Reposition the worksheet to the right of the Solver worksheet and modify the row labels and the column widths and other value-added features to improve the report's readability. Figure 16.5 is an example layout of the scenarios you have just created.

Table 16.5   Remodel Scenarios

Input cells	Scenario 1	Scenario 2	Scenario 3
Square feet	600	700	800
Addition	$130,600	$151,000	$172,000
Flooring	$ 9,500	$ 10,950	$ 12,250

Remodel Scenarios				
		600 SqFt	700 SqFt	800 SqFt
Changing Cells:				
	Square feet	600	700	800
	Addition	XXX	XXX	XXX
	Flooring	XXX	XXX	XXX
Price per square foot				
	Addition	$ 225.00	$ 215.71	$ 215.00
	Flooring	$ 15.83	$ 15.64	$ 15.31
	Loan Amount	$ 184,400	$201,850	$224,150

Notes: Current Values column represents values of changing cells at time Scenario Summary Report was created. Changing cells for each scenario are highlighted in gray.

Figure 16.5   Scenario Manager

▶ USING THE SPREADSHEET APPLICATION

On a new worksheet in the same workbook create a fifth worksheet, named AnswerSheet, for answering the following questions. Before answering each question reset the input values to their original values.

1. Jack and Susan are concerned about the price per square foot for the remodel.

    a. Assuming no changes in the costs in the seven remodel components, what would be the price per square foot for the addition if the square footage was increased to 800? For the flooring?

    b. What would be the percentage of the total cost of the Addition component if the contractor reduced the Addition cost to $120,000?

    c. Viewing the summary report, created with Scenario Manager, what is the difference of the Addition price per square foot between the 600 and 800 square foot scenarios? The difference of the Flooring price per square foot?

2. Jack and Susan are interested in using higher quality materials if the cost is not too prohibitive.

    a. What would be the Flooring cost they were willing to increase their flooring budget to 10% of the total remodeling cost? (Hint: Use Goal Seek.) Would this increased flooring budget exceed the $15,000, the limit of their initial upper limit for flooring? (Hint: See Data Validation.)

    b. Jack and Susan are willing to spend a maximum of $145,000 for the Addition component of the remodel. In that case, what is largest square footage they could consider so that the Addition price per square foot is $225?

3. Jack and Susan are considering the risk of borrowing up to $200,000 for the remodel.

    a. Viewing the Solver worksheet, what are the amounts they could spend on the Addition, Flooring, and Lighting components of the remodel?

    b. Use Solver to evaluate a new scenario with a maximum loan value of $200,000 changing only the tables, chairs, new oven, and wood-fired oven values. The constraints for each improvement need to be greater than or equal to the original amount. With the recommendations of Solver, what is the new percentage for chair cost?

4. Jack and Susan want to visualize the proportion of the remodel cost for all the remodel components other than the Addition component. Create a pie chart (from original values) depicting the percentage of cost for flooring, lighting, tables, chairs, new oven, and wood-fired oven. Apply some eye-appealing visual features to the chart. Viewing the chart, which component is the largest expense compared to the others?

5. Jack and Susan are thinking about the bank loan they will need to get for the remodel.

    a. What is their monthly payment for a 30-year loan if they borrow $195,000? (Hint: See the Data table.)

    b. What is their monthly payment for a 15-year loan if they were able to get a 5% rate on a $190,000 loan?

    c. Previously, they considered an 800 square foot addition (the third scenario saved in Scenario Manager). What is the monthly payment on that scenario's loan amount on a 30-year loan? On a 15-year loan?

Maxine's Travel Agency
Tour Financing

EXCEL WORKING CASE: ADVANCED LEVEL

Submission Instructions   Complete Case 17 in Excel. Answer the questions at the end of this case and insert the answers on an Answer Sheet in Case 17 Excel spreadsheet. Ask your instructor for submission instructions.

Preview   Maxine's Travel Agency specializes in planning international travel tours for retirees. The travel agency organizes large, all-inclusive tours, with available financing options. As the accountant in the billing department, you want to create a spreadsheet application to show clients different travel destinations, a breakdown of a trip's cost, and a table showing a customer's monthly payment depending on the cost of the tour.

Skill Set

PMT function
Data validation
Solver
Data table
Formula audit
Scenario manager

Background   Maxine's Travel Agency is located in Rio Rancho, New Mexico. Maxine has been booking travel tours for many years, specializing in the special travel needs of retirees. Maxine organizes tours of up to three weeks for groups of 20 to 40 people. Most of her customers like to travel to destinations in South America, Asia, and Europe. The travel agency provides all-inclusive travel packages that include domestic and international flights, most meals, lodging at 4-star hotels, and special excursions and attractions. They also provide the option to finance a trip with a monthly payment. The travel agency needs an easy-to-use spreadsheet application designed to show customers several travel options, including the various costs for each of the options and the payment options that are available. Maxine wants to interactively enter the tour information, such as number of people on the tour, number of days for the tour, and the various cost estimates for the tour including the flight, sightseeing, meals, and lodging.

Although the spreadsheet application should be flexible enough to plan for any tour, they want to initially use it to plan a group tour for the Retired Teachers Association. There are 35 people signed up for the tour and they want to explore options for traveling to South America, Thailand, Italy, and France. As the accountant you need to create a spreadsheet to show a summary of information for the four locations, as well as a payment table with monthly payment options. The Retired Teachers Association is working within a strict budget and needs to keep the cost for flights and hotels within a certain reasonable limit.

▶ CASE ANALYSIS

Output Requirements

Maxine has a good idea for a desired layout of the tour booking worksheet, as shown in Figure 17.1. The top portion of the layout shows the number of people on the tour, the name and costs of each tour option, and the cost per person and cost per group. The middle portion of the layout shows the monthly payment options. The bottom portion displays data tables showing a breakdown of a travel budget for possible tour cost amounts per person and per group.

Input Requirements

The 35 people in the Retired Teachers Association group are interested in four tour options, shown in Table 17.1.

You need to minimize the possibility of entering unreasonable cost estimates into the worksheet. Use the Data Validation tool to prevent certain data entry errors, as shown in Table 17.2.

Table 17.1 Tour Options

Location	Machu Picchu	Thailand	Italy	France
Tour name	Inca Trail	Beach Tour	Tour of Tuscany	Wine Country Tour
Number of days	10	14	12	14
Flight cost	$1,600	$900	$1,200	$1,200
Sightseeing package per day	$80	$50	$120	$150
Meals per day	$32	$27	$120	$135
Lodging per day	$100	$50	$150	$175

Table 17.2 Data Validation rules

Number of Guests on a Tour	Between 1-40
Number of Days for a Tour	Between 1-21

Maxine Travel Agency				
Tour Booking for: Retired Teaching Association				
Date				

Number of Guests on Tour	35		Interest Rate	3%

Location	Machu Picchu	Thailand	Italy	France
Tour Name	Inca Trail	Beach Tour	Tour of Tuscany	Wine Country Tour
Number of Days	10	14	12	14
Trip Costs				
Flight Cost	$ 1,600	$ 900	$ 1,200	$ 1,200
Sightseeing Package per Day	$ 80	$ 50	$ 120	$ 150
Meals per Day	$ 32	$ 27	$ 120	$ 135
Lodging Per Day	$ 100	$ 50	$ 150	$ 175
Total Cost Per Person				
Total Cost Per Group				
12 Monthly Payment Options				
Individual Payment				
Group Payment				

One Variable Table			One Variable Data Table	
Travel Budget Per Individual			**Travel Budget Per Group**	
Total Cost	Monthly Payment		Total Cost	Monthly Payment
$ 2,000.00	xxx		$ 80,000.00	xxx
$ 3,000.00	xxx		$ 90,000.00	xxx
$ 4,000.00	xxx		$ 100,000.00	xxx
$ 5,000.00	xxx		$ 110,000.00	xxx
$ 6,000.00	xxx		$ 120,000.00	xxx

◄ Tours / AnswerSheet / Machu Picchu Solver / Tuscany Solver / Tour Comparison / Tuscany S

Figure 17.1 Tour Booking Layout

Processing Requirements

Table 17.3 shows the required formulas you need to implement in the spreadsheet application.

To custom format cells for One Variable Data table headings:

1. Click on the cell that represents the Total cost of the tour in the Data table.
2. Using format cells, create a custom format to replace the total cost per person cell reference with the words "Total Cost".
3. Replace the individual monthly payment cell reference to the words "Monthly Payment".
4. Custom format the One Variable table. Travel Budget per Group using the same technique as above.

Table 17.3 Tour formulas

Feature	Formula
Total Cost Per Person	Flight Cost + (# of Days * Sightseeing) + (# of Days *Meals) + (# of Days * Lodging)
Total Cost Per Group	Total Cost Per Person * Number of people
Individual Monthly Payment Options	Use PMT function: Rate = (3% / 12), NPER = 12, PV = − (amount to be financed)
Group Monthly Payment Options	Use PMT function: Rate = (3% / 12), NPER = 12, PV = − (amount to be financed)
Travel Budget Per Guest One Variable Data table	Data table: reference cells are: total cost per guest and monthly payment per guest. Column input cell is increments of $1,000 starting at $2,000 and ending at $8,000. What-if Analysis: Data table column input cell is total cost per guest
Travel Budget Per Group One Variable Data Table	Data table: reference cells are: total cost per group and monthly payment per group. Column input cell is increments of $10,000 starting at $80,000 and ending in $200,000. What-if Analysis: Data table column input cell is total cost per group

▶ DESIGN AND IMPLEMENTATION

You want to design the spreadsheet application so you can quickly and accurately create multiple tour scenarios to help the clients make correct decisions.

Documentation

Using Figure 17.1 as your guide, apply appropriate value-added features to the title, section headings, and row labels. It is good design to indent the four trip cost items to visually differentiate them from the other row labels.

Input Area

Using Table 17.1 as your guide, verify the values of each of the four tour options. Use the Data Validation feature to designate valid data entry rules and alert messages.

Processing Area

Using Table 17.2 as your guide, enter the required formulas. First, enter the formulas to calculate the total cost per person and per group; then enter the payment option formulas. Use the Formula Auditing toolbar to verify the correct cells were used and that the Interest Rate cell was correctly used in the payment option formulas. Finally, create the two data tables. Make sure you correctly FORMAT all the numeric cells to make the worksheet easy to read.

▶ USING THE SPREADSHEET APPLICATION

In the workbook, create a second worksheet, named AnswerSheet, for answering the following questions. Before answering each question reset the input values to their original values.

1. Maxine and you are working with the Retired Teachers Association group. They keep changing their minds about various aspects of their travel requirements.

    a. What would be the total group amount for the Tuscany tour, if they decided that 20 people, instead of 35, will go on the tour?

    b. How large a group could take the Wine Country Tour in France if they had a budget of $300,000? (Hint: Use Goal Seek.) Would there be more people in the group than Maxine's group size limit?

    c. The group wants to consider the Thailand tour, but only if the total group cost is no more than $90,000. They would like to find less expensive lodging. What would be their lodging budget per person per night? (Hint: Use Goal Seek.)

2. The group would like a budget of $125,000 for the Machu Picchu trip with the following constraints. Using Solver, what are the results for lodging and sightseeing per day for a budget of $125,000?

    • Lodging (less than or equal to $200 a night)

    • Sightseeing (less than or equal to $100 a day)

    Save the answer report as a separate worksheet and rename the worksheet tab Machu Picchu Solver. Restore the original input data on the Tours worksheet.

3. The group would like a budget of $275,000 for the Tuscany trip with the following constraints. Using Solver, what are the results for lodging and sightseeing per day for a budget of $275,000?

    • Lodging (less than or equal to $300 a night)

    • Sightseeing (less than or equal to $200 a day)

    Save the answer report as a separate worksheet and rename the worksheet tab Tuscany Solver. Restore the original input data on the Tours worksheet.

4. The group would like a visualization comparing the total cost per person for the four tour destinations. Create an appropriate value-added clustered 2-D column chart; save the chart as a separate worksheet named Tour Comparison and position it to the right of the two Solver worksheets.

5. The group is concerned with the 12-month financing options offered by Maxine's Travel Agency.

    a. Viewing the data tables, what is the difference in an individual's monthly payment between financing $3,000 and $5,000? In the group's monthly payment between financing $100,000 and $160,000?

    b. How much would the monthly payment increase for each person on the Thailand tour if you increased the interest rate to 5%?

6. The group is seriously thinking about the Tuscany tour. They are considering three scenarios. Use Scenario Manager to create the Tuscany scenarios with the data shown below. Then create a scenario report showing the scenarios' total cost per person and per group. Position the report worksheet to the right of the other worksheets in the workbook, name it Tuscany Scenarios, and make the appropriate value-added modifications.

Scenario Name	10-Day	15-Day	21-Day
Number of Days	10	15	21
Sightseeing Package per Day	$90	$120	$100
Meals per Day	$120	$110	$90
Lodging per Day	$150	$175	$110

a. Select the 15-Day scenario. What is the individual monthly payment? The group monthly payment?

b. Switch between the 10-Day and 21-Day scenarios. What is the difference in the total cost per person between the two scenarios? The difference in the total group cost?

c. Which scenario do you consider the best deal?

7. The travel agency makes a profit by financing the tours.

a. How much money in interest is the travel agency making from the France trip? Calculate profit from the group price.

b. What is the profit from interest for the Italy trip if you made the payment plan for two years instead of one year? Calculate profit from the group price.

c. As the accountant, would you recommend the one-year financing or the two-year financing? Explain the risks and benefits involved in your decision.

Thomas Paul Investment, Inc.
Property Investment Analysis
EXCEL WORKING CASE: ADVANCED LEVEL

Submission Instructions   Complete Case 18 in Excel. Answer the questions at the end of this case and insert the answers on an Answer Sheet in the Case 18 Excel spreadsheet. Ask your instructor for submission instructions.

Preview   Thomas Paul Investment, Inc., purchases residential real estate for short-term investment and/or rental income. The company's main purpose is to carry out minor repairs, lease the properties, and eventually sell them for a profit. As a real estate investor for the company, you want to create a spreadsheet application to analyze and compare the costs associated with each of three properties and to decide which two of the three properties would be the best investments.

Skill Set

PMT function
Data validation
Solver
Data table
Formula audit
Scenario manager

Background   Thomas Paul Investment, Inc., purchases residential real estate for short-term investment and/or rental income. The investment company owns more than 200 rental properties across the United States and is interested in purchasing two properties in San Diego County, California. The company has narrowed their search to three properties. You need to develop a spreadsheet application to analyze and compare the costs associated with each of the three properties and to decide which two of the three properties would be the best investments.

Thomas Paul Investment considers two key factors in their real estate investment decisions: total monthly expenses and net profit. These two values are calculated based on estimated annual expenses for the property and various assumptions based on averages of previous purchases within the area. The company does not want to spend more than a certain annual amount for a particular property. You need to use the spreadsheet application to enter the purchase information for each of the properties, calculate the various expenses and profit for the properties, modify the values of assumptions to evaluate the what-if analysis, and show reports and charts summarizing information for the three investment options.

▶ CASE ANALYSIS

Output Requirements

The investment analysis worksheet should include information on the properties being considered, the assumptions, and a data table of monthly payments associated with different purchase prices, as shown in Figure 18.1.

Input Requirements

Thomas Paul Investment uses assumed values for several variables in their analysis, as shown in Table 18.1.

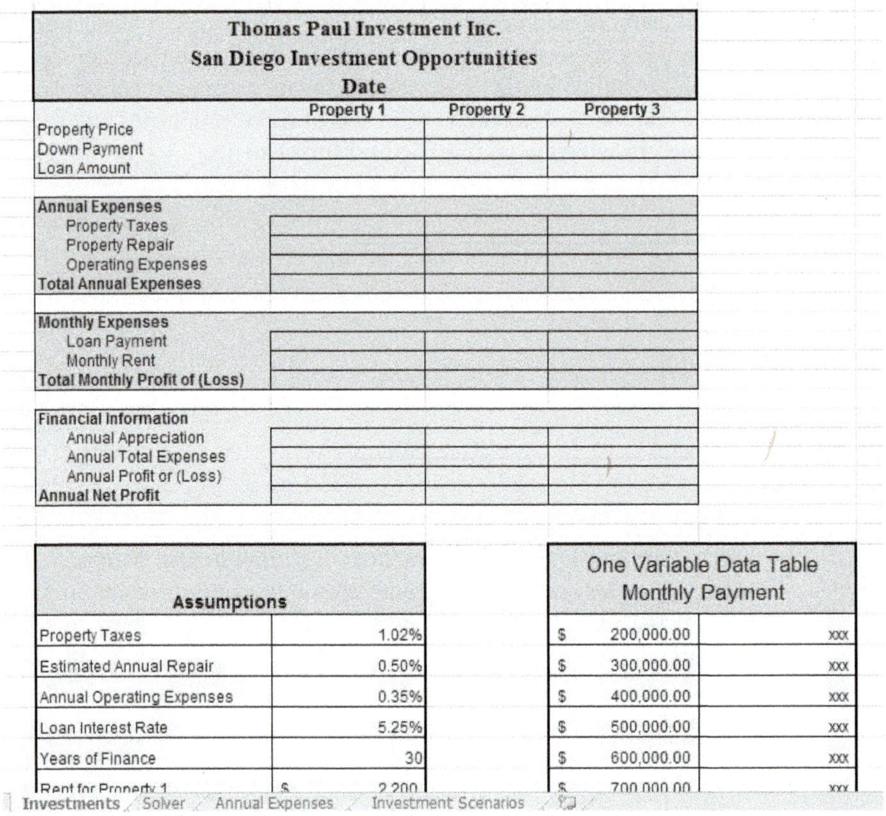

Thomas Paul Investment Inc.
San Diego Investment Opportunities
Date

	Property 1	Property 2	Property 3
Property Price			
Down Payment			
Loan Amount			
Annual Expenses			
Property Taxes			
Property Repair			
Operating Expenses			
Total Annual Expenses			
Monthly Expenses			
Loan Payment			
Monthly Rent			
Total Monthly Profit of (Loss)			
Financial Information			
Annual Appreciation			
Annual Total Expenses			
Annual Profit or (Loss)			
Annual Net Profit			

Assumptions		One Variable Data Table	Monthly Payment
Property Taxes	1.02%	$ 200,000.00	xxx
Estimated Annual Repair	0.50%	$ 300,000.00	xxx
Annual Operating Expenses	0.35%	$ 400,000.00	xxx
Loan Interest Rate	5.25%	$ 500,000.00	xxx
Years of Finance	30	$ 600,000.00	xxx
Rent for Property 1	$ 2,200	$ 700,000.00	xxx

Investments / Solver / Annual Expenses / Investment Scenarios /

Figure 18.1 Investment Analysis Layout

Table 18.1   Investment Assumptions

Assumptions Table	
Variable	Value
Price for property 1	$300,000
Price for property 2	$450,000
Price for property 3	$500,000
Down payment	10%
Property taxes	1.02%
Estimated annual repair	0.50%
Annual operating expenses	0.35%
Loan interest rate	5.25%
Years of finance	30
Rent for property 1	$2,200 per month
Rent for property 2	$2,500 per month
Rent for property 3	$2,800 per month
Average equity increase per year	0.40%

Although these values are used to calculate the profit for a property, the company likes to do what-if analysis by changing some of these initial values as desired. The company wants to reduce data entry errors as much as possible and needs the worksheet designed to prevent unreasonable assumed values, as shown in Table 18.2.

Processing Requirements

Table 18.3 shows the required formulas to be implemented in the spreadsheet application.

► DESIGN AND IMPLEMENTATION

You want to design the spreadsheet application so you can quickly and accurately create multiple scenarios so you can confidently decide on the best property investment option.

Documentation

Using Figure 18.1 as your guide, apply appropriate value-added features to the title, section headings, and row labels. Use bold text and indentation to visually differentiate the group titles, such as Annual Expenses, from their category titles, such as Property Taxes and Property Repair. Use color shading to help the spreadsheet user differentiate the various sections of the spreadsheet.

Table 18.2   Data Validation Entry Rules

Down Payment	Greater than 0% and less than or equal to 12%
Loan Interest Rate	Greater than 0% and less than or equal to 7%

Table 18.3 Workbook formulas

Feature	Formula
Down Payment	Property Price $*$ Down Payment %
Loan Amount	Property Price $-$ Down Payment
Annual Property Taxes	Property Price $*$ Property Tax Rate
Annual Property Repair	Property Price $*$ Estimated Annual Repair
Annual Operating Expenses	Property Price $*$ Annual Operating Expense
Total Annual Expenses	Sum function of all Annual Expenses
Monthly Loan Payment	PMT Function. See Assumptions table for PMT information.
Monthly Rent	See Assumptions table for Property rent values, enter the cell reference from the Assumptions table.
Total MOnthly Profit or (Loss)	Monthly Rent $-$ Monthly Loan Payment
Annual Appreciation	Property Price $*$ Annual Appreciation
Annual Total Expenses	Enter a cell reference for the Total Annual Expenses.
Annual Profit or (Loss)	Total Monthly Profit or (Loss) $*$ 12
Annual Net Profit	(Annual Appreciation + Annual Profit or (Loss)) $-$ Annual Total Expenses
One Variable Data Table	Data Table Reference Cells are: Loan Amount and Monthly Payment. The column input cell values are Loan Amount increments of $100,000 starting with $200,000 and ending at $900,000.

To custom format cells for Data table headings:

1. Click on the cell that represents the loan payment within the Data table.
2. Use Format Cells to create a custom format to replace the loan payment cell reference with the words Loan Amount.
3. Use quotations within your custom format.
4. Create the Loan Amount heading.

Input Area

Using Table 18.2 as your guide, verify the values of the three value of Property Price and the values in the Assumptions table. Use the Data Validation feature to designate the valid data entry rules and alert messages as shown in Table 18.2.

Processing Area

Using Table 18.3 as your guide, enter the required formulas. Make sure you correctly enter each of the assumption (parameter) cell addresses in the appropriate formulas. Use the Formula Auditing toolbar to verify the correct cells were used in each of the formulas. After verifying the formulas, create the Monthly Payment data table using the information in Table 18.3. Make sure you correctly format all the numeric cells to make the worksheet easy to read.

► USING THE SPREADSHEET APPLICATION

In the workbook, create a second worksheet, named AnswerSheet, for answering the following questions. Before answering each question reset the input values to their original values.

1. As the real estate investor, you want to consider the three options with the current assumptions.

   a. Which of the three properties seems the best investment?

   b. Considering the initial investment for Property 1 is $300,000 what is the profit margin percentage based on annual net profit if the loan was paid off?

   c. Property 2 and Property 3 are relatively expensive and, with the current assumptions, have negative annual net profits. Examining the worksheet, which variables seem to contribute the most to the negative profit values?

2. You are seriously evaluating Property 1 but want to control expenses and be able to charge a reasonable rent. You want an Annual Net Profit of $6,000 for the property, under the conditions that Property Repair is kept to $1,000 or less, that Operating Expenses are limited to no more than $1,200, and that Monthly Rent is less than or equal to $2,500. Use Solver to show the resultant report. Position the report's worksheet to the right of the Investments worksheet.

   a. Are the values for this set of conditions reasonable?

   b. Modify the section headings and row labels in the solver report, and enhance the solver report's title to improve the readability of the report.

3. You are presenting your analysis to colleagues and need to visualize the annual expenses of the three properties. Use the Chart Wizard to create a 2-D Column Chart comparing the three types of annual expenses for the three properties. Insert a chart title and other appropriate value-added features. Save the chart as a separate worksheet named Annual Expenses and position it to the right of the Solver worksheet. Studying the annual expense chart, describe the similarities and differences of the properties' annual expenses.

4. As the real estate investor, you like the location of Property 2 and want to explore how to purchase it and at least break even annually, that is, have an annual net profit of at least $1.

   a. You can afford to change the Down Payment percentage. Can you increase the down payment percentage without going over the company's limit (see Table 18.1) and break even?

   b. You are a decent negotiator and are talking with the seller of Property 2. You agree to pay a 12% down payment. What property price and down payment would allow you to break even, all other variables staying the same? (Hint: Use Goal Seek.)

5. Property 3 is in very good shape and at a very desirable location, but is really expensive. However, it would be good if Thomas Paul Investment were able to have some high-end properties in its portfolio.

   a. What would be the annual net profit for Property 3 if you could get a loan interest rate of 3%, make a 12% down payment, and have estimated annual repairs of just .2%? Would this be a desirable scenario?

   b. Is the above-mentioned scenario desirable for Property 2?

   c. Given the above-mentioned scenario, does it make any sense to have a 25-year loan instead of a 30-year loan?

6. You are considering three scenarios: a very affordable, low-risk investment scenario, a reasonable investment scenario, and an expensive, risky, investment scenario. Use Scenario Manager to create the three investment scenarios with the data shown below; also create a scenario for the original assumptions, as shown below. Then create a scenario report showing the four scenarios' annual net profit. Position the report worksheet to the right of the other worksheets in the workbook, name it Investment Scenarios, and make the appropriate value-added modifications.

Scenario Name (Changing Cells)	Affordable	Reasonable	Expensive	Original
Down payment	5%	9%	12%	10%
Loan interest rate	3%	4%	4.5%	5.25%
Appreciation	0.20%	.030%	0.40%	0.40%

   a. Show the Reasonable scenario. What are the monthly loan payments for the three properties? Based on the monthly loan payment, which property is a better investment?

   b. The property rental market is strong and you want to offer competitive monthly rental rates on your properties. Show the Expensive scenario. For Property 3, what monthly rental could you charge and have an annual net profit of $10,000? (Hint: Use Goal Seek.)

   c. Show the Original Assumptions scenario to reset to the initial values.

7. Studying the Investment Scenarios report, you realize a visualization of the results would be helpful to your colleagues. Create a column chart comparing the annual net profit for each Affordable, Reasonable, and Expensive scenarios for the three properties. Save the chart directly below the investment scenario on the same worksheet. Make sure you design a title, appropriate axis titles, and other appropriate value-added features.

PART III

DEVELOPING A WEBSITE APPLICATION

A website application is a software tool to present information over the Internet to meet the needs of groups of people. A particular website is a collection of information (web pages) about the various topics that comprise the overall purpose and objectives of the website. Each web page is organized to present the content clearly and concisely. The web pages are organized to make it easy to navigate among them. Website applications are important tools for communicating electronically with an organization's customers.

You should follow a three-phase approach to create a website application: analysis, design, and implementation.

In the *analysis phase*, you need to understand as well as you can the intended purpose of the website application, especially the information needs and expectations of the intended users of the website. You need to identify the website's topical content and the overall content structure, usually a hierarchy of topics. You need to think about an intuitive, easy-to-understand navigation scheme among the web pages. You need to identify the desired look and feel for the website as a whole. Each of the following cases presents the website's requirements; in the real world you determine these requirements through interviews with intended users of the website application.

In the *design phase*, you need to decide how to lay out the web pages' content and navigation menus. A well-designed website is easy to use and presents high-quality content. There are many design guidelines you can follow to make sure the content is clearly written and the website is easy to navigate. These design guidelines are discussed briefly as you go through the website cases.

During the *implementation phase* you use an HTML, or web page, editor to create the web pages that make up the website. In the following website cases, you may use the HTML editor of your choice to create the web pages, the navigation menus, and value-added design features to improve the usability of the website application. You should verify that each web page communicates the intended content clearly, that all the navigation hyperlinks work properly, and that the intended look and feel of the website is consistent for all the web pages.

CHAPTER 7

Website Design

Up the Hill Bakery
Customer-Oriented Website

WEBSITE DESIGN TEACHING CASE

Submission Instructions Complete Case 19. Answer the questions at the end of this case and ask your instructor for submission instructions.

Preview You have been hired as a Web designer to create a website for the bakery. The owners want to provide online access to information about Up the Hill Bakery for their current customers and to attract new customers. They want the website to show relevant information about the bakery, and they want it to be customer friendly and easy to use. They would like the page design to have a French look and feel similar to their bakery.

Skill Set

Relative Links	Absolute Links
Table with borders	Page formats
Page Titles	Insert image
Folder hierarchy	Design concepts

Background Jack and his wife Susan (yes, they are still married!) have built a good reputation for their small French bakery in Chula Vista, California. Their customers—local residents and other small restaurants—consistently rate the bakery the Best Bakery in local magazine surveys. They have recently expanded the bakery's restaurant capacity for serving breakfast and lunch and have upgraded their ovens to provide a wider variety of fresh breads and pastries. They want to enhance the bakery's competitive advantage by providing an easy way to serve existing customers and to attract new customers.

Jack and Susan want you to develop a straightforward design for a website they can use to market their business on the Internet. They want the website to show as much information about the bakery as feasible, but they also want to have a good-looking website that is easy for customers to understand and use.

► CASE ANALYSIS

Output Requirements

The owners of the bakery would like the website to show a description and price for bread and pastry items, list the breakfast and lunch menus, include delivery information, and provide administrative information, such as the bakery's address, phone number, and driving directions to the bakery. The owners would also like a specific page for the recipe of the day. Jack and Susan are eager to have a well-designed website; they have used other companies' websites and have complained that the organizations of these sites are sometimes confusing, and they often get lost when they are trying to find the information they want. Also, their bakery has a French theme and they want the website to communicate visually an appropriate style and image to customers.

Input Requirements

Table 19.1 shows the items for sale in the bakery.

Processing Requirements

Jack and Susan intend their website to be an electronic brochure that provides access to the bakery's information. If customers like the website, Jack and Susan will consider including the processing support for customers to make purchases online.

Table 19.1   Menu Items

Breakfast Items	Lunch Items	Bread Items	Pastries
French toast	Gratinée d'oignon	Olive bread	Almond brown butter
Scrambled eggs with	(French onion soup)	Raisin bread	cake
salmon	Plateau de Fromage	Rye bread	Tiramisu
Egg & cheese	Oven Roasted	Sourdough	S'mores
croissant	Chicken	French baguettes	Black velvet cake
Strawberry & cream	Duck Breast Salad	Sundried tomato	7-Layer chocolate
crepes	Quiche Lorraine	focaccia	cake
Brioche with egg and	Crêpe Au Crabe (crab		Gala apple pie
spinach	crêpe)		
Lemon and walnut			
pancakes			

► DESIGN AND IMPLEMENTATION

Web Page Layout

Design Principle

The pages of a well-designed website have a consistent, grid-like layout scheme that includes a title area, a content area, a navigation menu, an area for other information, and a font and color format. A well-designed, consistent layout of a website's pages increases users' ease of reading and understanding the content and navigation and their satisfaction with the site. You can design and save a web file (an HTML file) with all the desired common design features of the website's pages and then use the file as a template to design and implement each of the actual pages, adding and modifying the content and navigation hyperlinks as needed. Figure 19.1 shows a straightforward web page layout.

Implementation

Use the web page editor of your choice to create a web page layout file (an HTML file) relevant for the Up the Hill Bakery website.

Website Content Organization

Design Principle

A good organizational design for a website's content is a hierarchy of web pages, as shown in Figure 19.2. The first, or top, page is the website's home page, providing the user with an orientation to the purpose and overall content of the website. The second

Page Title	
Navigation Menu Internal Hyperlinks External Hyperlinks	Information Content Area
Other Information	

Figure 19.1 Generic Web page Layout

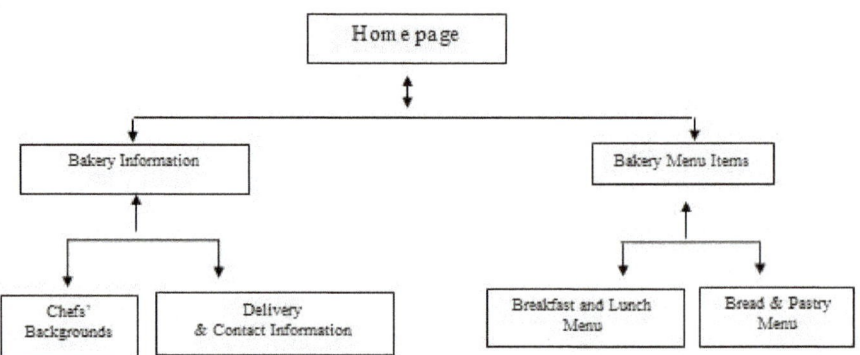

Figure 19.2   Generic Website Hierarchical Structure

level of the hierarchy comprises the web pages for each of any number of topics of the website, as shown in Figure 19.2 with three topics. If a topic is sufficiently complex, the content should be subdivided into an appropriate number of subtopics, each a separate page, represented by the third hierarchy level in Figure 19.2.

The content in each web page needs to be written appropriately, providing the website's users with essential, relevant information and avoiding information overload. The writing style should be frugal and to the point, with text composed in short paragraphs and with bulleted lists and tables used where appropriate. Relevant graphics, such as charts, maps, clip art, and photos, should be used to support the content of the page. Each page's overall visual design should be balanced, with each design element in proportion, so that the user can easily find and read the content on the computer screen.

The next section discusses navigation links among the pages (shown as arrows in Figure 19.2) and to other websites.

Website Content Organization

Implementation

1. Create a home page to include the bakery's name and any other information you think would be useful, such as a photo of the bakery, a short history of the bakery, and culinary awards achieved by the bakery.
2. Create a breakfast and lunch menu page. Edit the title area appropriately, and edit the content area to include several breakfast and lunch items that are listed in Figure 19.1.
3. Create a bread and pastry item page. Edit the title area appropriately, and edit the content area to include several types of breads and pastries found in Figure 19.1. Use a table feature to organize the descriptions of the items and their prices, and provide appropriate bread or pastry images.

4. Create a bakery information page. Edit the title area appropriately, and edit the content area to describe the bakery's delivery service, including mileage charges, times of delivery, and minimum amount to deliver. Include a section that provides the address, driving directions, phone number, and hours of operation.

5. Create a chef background page. Edit the title area appropriately, and edit the content area to include text of brief interviews with the chefs. Use a table feature to organize the brief paragraphs and photos for the chefs.

Website Navigation

Design Principle

Hypertext links, or hyperlinks, are used to create navigational paths among the pages of a website and to pages of other websites. The overall navigational features of a website need to be clear and consistent to prevent confusion. The navigational paths in a website with a hierarchical design, as shown in Figure 19.2, should allow the user to go from a web page to web pages up and down the hierarchy within the same topic, horizontally on the same level of the hierarchy within a topic, and back to the home page; these hyperlinks should be arranged as a menu, or list, consistently on each web page, as shown in Figure 19.1. Hyperlinks to pages in other websites can be arranged in a menu structure, or a single such hyperlink can be placed appropriately in the page's information content area.

Implementation

1. Include a navigation bar with relative links on your home page to include two links: Bakery Information and Bakery Menu Items.

2. Include a secondary navigation bar on the Bakery Information page for links to Chefs' Backgrounds, Delivery, and Contact Information (see Figure 19.2).

3. Include an additional secondary navigation bar on the Bakery Items page for hyperlinks to the breakfast and lunch menu and the bread and pastry menu (see Figure 19.2).

4. Include two absolute links (outside links). These can be outside links for special interests that pertain to the business.

5. Include an e-mail link.

► USING THE WEBSITE APPLICATION

1. When you decide to publish, what do you save as your first page?

2. To support your website and the bakery's success it is a good idea to create a Facebook business page. What are some other ways you can drive business using social commerce?

3. Name three blog sites you can use to create a blog for the bakery.

4. What is the difference between a static website and a dynamic one?

5. When you decide to publish your site, what are some of the first steps in doing so?

Bella Spa

Customer-Oriented Website

WEBSITE DESIGN WORKING CASE

Submission Instructions   Complete Case 20. Answer the questions at the end of this case and ask your instructor for submission instructions.

Preview   You are a web designer and have been paid to design a website for Bella Day Spa. This website should be customer friendly and should include as much information as possible about the day spa, the products and services they provide, and contact information.

Skill Set

Relative Links	Absolute Links
Table with borders	Page formats
Page Titles	Insert image
Folder hierarchy	Design concepts

Background   Bella Day Spa is a full service spa that just opened in the heart of the main square of Santa Fe, New Mexico. The owners want you to design a website so that customers can see what different spa packages are available and the price list for these services. The owners want a website that is easy to use and has the look and feel of the spa's southwest ambience.

▶ CASE ANALYSIS

Output Requirements

The Bella Day Spa owners want the website to include contact information and information about various spa treatments and their new line body care products. They would like this information arranged as a hierarchy of four or more web pages, organized with appropriate menu navigation among the web pages and with appropriate hyperlinks to other relevant spa-oriented websites. The owners are open to your ideas about the website's design, but they definitely want a consistent web page layout and they want the website overall to be aesthetically pleasing and easy to navigate.

Input Requirements

Box 20.1 shows some of the spa information the owners want to include on a web page. You will create the remaining information regarding the following on your own.

- Welcome page
- Contact information (address, phone number, etc.)
- Driving directions
- Spa information (see Box 20.1)
- Spa service page: various spa treatments
- Spa product page: body care products
- A relevant title for each page
- Links that allow the user to navigate to all pages
- Consistent design
- At least one e-mail link
- At least one outside website link (make sure this is relevant to the site, not just a random link)
- At least one table with rows and columns
- Images in your site as needed

▶ DESIGN AND IMPLEMENTATION

Web Page Layout

Design Principle

The web pages need to have a consistent layout and color scheme. Consider an appropriate layout for the Bella Day Spa.

Implementation

Use the web page editor of your choice to create a web page layout file (an HTML file) relevant for the Bella Day Spa website.

Box 20.1 Spa Hours and Facilities

- Hours of Operation: 7:00 AM to 7:00 PM
- Men's locker room with steam room and showers
- Women's locker room with steam room and showers
- Hot tub in each locker room
- Relaxation room that serves fresh fruits and exotic teas
- Cold plunge pool
- 18% gratuity included
- Arrive 20 minutes before service
- Free parking for up to 2 hours

Website Content Organization

Design Principle

A website's content organized in a hierarchy structure is easy to use. The breadth and depth of the hierarchy depends on the complexity of the information and the needs of the users. The amount of content on a web page should be somewhat limited, preferably to the size of a computer screen so the user does not have to scroll. Consider the information content for the Bella Day Spa and an appropriate hierarchy structure.

Implementation

1. Create a welcome (home) page and include contact information and driving directions on the page.
2. Create a Spa Information page with content shown in Box 20.1.
3. Create a Spa Services page with content for at least five spa treatments, their descriptions, and their prices. Use a tabular layout to organize the treatment information on the page. Include appropriate images where desired.
4. Create a Products page with content for at least five items, their descriptions, and their prices.

Website Navigation

Design Principle

The navigation menu(s) should be located consistently on all the web pages so users can quickly navigate the website without wasting time searching for the hyperlinks. The hyperlinks are usually designed as text—a word or short phrase—but images, especially icons, may be used as hyperlinks when appropriate.

Implementation

1. Edit the Welcome page to show the appropriate navigation links in the menu. Include one or more absolute links to appropriate spa-oriented websites; do not use the actual URL address of the website as the hyperlink text.
2. Edit the menus for the Spa Information page, the Spa Services page, and the Products page. Include hyperlinks to appropriate websites, where desired.

▶ USING THE WEBSITE APPLICATION

1. Create a Twitter account: Use your Name, Case20, Bella Spa. Have your instructor sign up as one of the followers. Tweet a special spa treatment of the day and send it to your followers.
2. What are the two most popular software packages for designing websites?
3. What is the average cost to host a simple website?
4. Name a company that hosts websites.
5. What is the average price to buy a domain name?

Legends

Sports Memorabilia Website

WEBSITE DESIGN WORKING CASE

Submission Instructions Complete Case 21. Answer the questions at the end of this case and ask your instructor for submission instructions.

Preview You have been hired as a web designer to design a site for Legends, a sports memorabilia online store. The website should be customer friendly and include different categories of sports memorabilia for sale. The owner also needs you to design a page that updates the customer on payment and shipment information.

Skill Set

Relative Links	Absolute Links
Table with borders	Page formats
Page Titles	Insert image
Folder hierarchy	Design concepts

Background Mike Nitsch is a sports nut, fascinated especially with the traditions and history of athletic competition, both professional and amateur. Mike is creating a business plan for a new online business for marketing sports memorabilia. He wants you to create a prototype design of a website for his new e-commerce business, named Legends. Mike wants a well-designed website that emphasizes ease of use by customers.

▶ CASE ANALYSIS

Output Requirements

Mike wants the Legends website to support sales of many different kinds of sports memorabilia from many different types of sports. He wants the website's content to clearly show the various memorabilia products for each of the sports, along with purchasing information. He wants the information arranged in an appropriate hierarchy of web pages, with appropriate menu navigation among the pages and hyperlinks to sports-related websites. Mike wants you to develop your ideas for the overall website's design, but he insists that the web pages' layout be consistent, aesthetically pleasing, and easy to navigate.

Input Requirements

Box 21.1 shows purchasing information that you need to include in the web page. The owner is interested in all sports, but he definitely wants to market baseball, football, and golf memorabilia on the website.

- Create a Welcome page.
- Include an orientation to the general topic of sports memorabilia and contact information.
- Create a Payment and Shipping web page with content shown in Box 21.1.
- Create three Product web pages, one each for baseball, football, and golf. On each of the three web pages include content for at least five memorabilia items for sale. Provide a short description of the items, the prices, and weight of each item.
- Give a relevant title for each page.
- Include links that allow the user to navigate to all pages.
- Use a consistent design.
- Provide at least one e-mail link.
- Provide at least one outside website link (make sure this is relevant to the site, not just a random link).
- Include at least one table with rows and columns.
- Use images within your site as needed.

▶ DESIGN AND IMPLEMENTATION

Web Page Layout

Design Principle

Customers expect to see web pages that have a consistent layout, with design features such as the page title, navigation menu, and content area in the same location on each of the web pages. Using a grid layout ensures a consistent design. Consider an appropriate web page layout for the Legends website.

Box 21.1   Purchasing Information

- Accepts payment from MasterCard, Visa, and PayPal
- Delivery cost is by weight
- Delivery is by UPS
- Returns must be within 14 days of receiving shipment
- 15% restocking fee for all returned items

Implementation

Use the web page editor of your choice to create a web page layout file (an HTML file) relevant to the Legends website.

Website Content Organization

Design Principle

A website's content comprises many topics, all related to the main theme, or purpose, of the website. Considering the idea of an outline, each topic's content should be organized on one or more web pages in a hierarchy structure. The users of a website expect the content on each page to be highly legible and easy to scan visually. Design features such as text alignment, white space, font style and size, and concise prose should be used to increase a web page's readability. Consider the information content for the Legends website and an appropriate hierarchy structure.

Implementation

1. Create a home page. Include an orientation to the general topic of sports memorabilia and contact information.
2. Create a Payment and Shipping web page with the content shown in Box 21.1.
3. Create three Product web pages, one each for baseball, football, and golf. On each of the three pages include content for at least five memorabilia items for sale. Provide a short description of the items, the price, and weight of each item. Use a grid layout to organize the information on the page. Include appropriate images where needed.

Website Navigation

Design Principle

The hyperlinks to navigate among the various pages in the website should be designed as a vertical or horizontal menu, placed consistently on each web page. The hyperlinks to other websites may be placed in the menu as well or appropriately placed in the content area of the web page.

Implementation

Edit the Welcome page to show the appropriate navigation links in the menu. Include one or more absolute links to appropriate sports-oriented websites; do not use the URL of the website as the hyperlink text. Edit the menus for each of the Product web pages. Include hyperlinks to appropriate sports-oriented websites, where desired.

► USING THE WEBSITE APPLICATION

1. Create a blog using WordPress.org. Include an introductory page, using the same information as the introductory page on your website. Create the WordPress blog under your name and send your instructor the link once you have finished.
2. Include a baseball video from youtube.com in your blog.
3. Why is it a good idea to create a blog for your company as well as a website?
4. What is f-commerce? What is l-commerce?